# INTRODUCTION TO BLOCK 5

*Written for the course team by Fiona Richards*

At this stage in the course you have encountered all of the eight disciplines which go to make up A103, and have also undertaken some interdisciplinary study. Your work in Block 5 will revisit some of the disciplines studied in Blocks 1 and 2, but will now draw these disciplines together into an interdisciplinary block of study, the title of which is 'Myths and Conventions'. The disciplines contributing to Block 5 are Classical Studies, Literature and Music.

## Texts and approaches

Each week of study introduces you to one main text. You will start by reading a dramatic text, George Bernard Shaw's *Pygmalion*. Weeks 20 and 21 are both devoted to another, much earlier, dramatic text, an English translation of Euripides' *Medea*. Week 22 will reintroduce you to music, with a case study of Richard Strauss's orchestral work *Don Juan*, and Block 5 concludes with a novel, Jean Rhys's *Wide Sargasso Sea*.

Whilst you will be studying texts drawn from different disciplines and from different historical periods, the teaching of these texts shares common methods and common themes. The method of study common to all five units that make up this block is that you will examine one core text in some detail, with attention given to close reading. You will also look at the historical context of the texts concerned, developing the work begun in Block 3. As part of the study process you will spend some time getting to grips with the technical language and vocabulary appropriate to each of the texts.

There are a number of common themes which give coherence to the block, although not all these themes are covered in every unit (and indeed some are more relevant than others to certain units). The themes are:

(i) the reworking of myths;

(ii) the representation of character and gender;

(iii) traditions and conventions, in forms and meanings, and the ways in which these conventions have been challenged by writers and composers;

(iv) drama and performance.

These are all themes that are often addressed in modern critical approaches to the Arts, as is the idea of alienation and related topics such as madness and exile, which are explored in *Medea* and *Wide Sargasso Sea*. You will also consider the interpretation of texts by watching

A(ZX)103

**An Introduction to the Humanities**

The Open University

# Myths and Conventions

Block 5

This publication forms part of an Open University course A(ZX)103 *An Introduction to the Humanities*. Details of this and other Open University courses can be obtained from the Student Registration and Enquiry Service, The Open University, PO Box 197, Milton Keynes, MK7 6BJ, United Kingdom: tel.+44 (0)870 333 4340, email general-enquiries@open.ac.uk

Alternatively, you may visit the Open University website at http://www.open.ac.uk where you can learn more about the wide range of courses and packs offered at all levels by The Open University

To purchase a selection of Open University course materials visit http://www.open.ac.uk, or contact Open University Worldwide, Michael Young Building, Walton Hall, Milton Keynes MK7 6AA, United Kingdom for a brochure. tel. +44 (0)1908 858785; fax +44 (0)1908 858787; e-mail ouwenq@open.ac.uk

The Open University
Walton Hall, Milton Keynes
MK7 6AA

First published 1998. Second edition 2005.

Edited and designed by The Open University.

Typeset by The Open University.

Printed and bound in the United Kingdom by CPI, Bath.

ISBN 0 7492 9669 0

2.1

31612B/a103b5i3.1

different performances of *Medea* and by reading a selection of criticisms of the texts in the block.

## The reworking of myths

One of the themes of Block 5 is myth, and in particular the ways in which traditional myths survive and are refashioned. The word 'myth' in English means (broadly speaking) two contradictory things: first, a story that is widely believed but not true, and second, a story that everybody knows is not real, but which expresses powerful truths. Myths, legends and other familiar tales tend to be retold when the reteller sees in them something of relevance to his or her own times or situation. Thus, Shaw's reworking of Ovid's tale of how the statue of a woman is brought to life is relevant to the suffragette movement of his day, whilst Euripedes alters the story of Medea for his own dramatic purposes. Strauss's adaptation of the Don Juan myth is a very personal undertaking, intended partly as a reflection of his own romantic situation, and *Wide Sargasso Sea* reworks a gothic myth familiar in horror stories, the vengeful madwoman hidden in the attic. TV22 looks at the traditional Scottish myth of a mortal who is stolen or who disappears, and the ways in which this myth is reworked in musical terms by composer Judith Weir.

## Character and gender

Each of the five units of Block 5 focuses on the representation of character, whether through dramatic dialogue, within a novel or in musical language. The sorts of question that will be addressed are:

Who are the characters involved, and what means does the author or composer use to depict them?

How do characters communicate or interact?

How are men and women portrayed?

Does their portrayal accord with stereotype gender differences?

How do characters express emotions?

How are characters presented within a narrative?

## Traditions and conventions

Each of the works chosen for study in Block 5 conforms to conventions. For example, Shaw's *Pygmalion* employs a traditional dramatic structure, which is related to the classical legacy. Similarly, some of the conventions of Greek drama can be seen at work in *Medea*. But each of the texts we will study also challenges conventions in some way, whether in terms of the formal structure of the work in question or in terms of its content.

Richard Strauss changes a traditional musical structure into a narrative vehicle, and Euripides abandons some of the conventional male/female roles. *Wide Sargasso Sea* simultaneously challenges the conventions of realist narrative and produces a striking experiment with the interplay of different fictional voices.

## Drama and performance

The first three units of Block 5 are devoted to two dramatic texts. You will therefore spend some time considering the nature of a dramatic text and its realization in performance. You will consider performance issues such as the use of space, gesture, expression, stance, costume and scenery. Complete performances of both *Pygmalion* and *Medea* are included on audio-cassette, and performance material relating to *Medea* also appears in TV20 and TV21. With both these texts, questions of dramatic form and convention will be discussed, and the units will consider how differences of gender and differences of class are coded and conveyed in dramatic dialogue.

## Assessment

Your work in Block 5 is assessed by way of an interdisciplinary essay, TMA07. The subject of the essay will be related to one of the themes discussed above, and will require you to discuss more than one text. You are therefore advised to bear in mind the themes of the block as you work through each of the units.

# UNIT 19
# STUDYING
# *PYGMALION*

*Written for the course team by Cicely Palser Havely*

## Contents

| STUDY COMPONENTS | | | | |
|---|---|---|---|---|
| Weeks of study | Texts | TV | AC | Set books |
| 1 | *Resource Book 3* | TV19 | AC6 AC7 | *Pygmalion* |

## Aims

The aims of this unit are:

1   to continue your introduction to literary studies by showing you some aspects of the nature and forms of drama;

2   to study a well-regarded and popular example in context;

3   to introduce the particular thematic concerns of this block: *myth* and *convention*, and other key terms for studying the humanities, including *gender, tradition, performance* and *interpretation*.

This will be achieved by listening to a whole play, and then (once some introductory questions have been raised) returning to each act in turn to investigate certain aspects of drama in general and the play in particular, side by side.

## Study note: planning your study time

Section 1 will take longest, because it includes listening to a whole play. The other four sections should each take 2–3 hours.

# 1 INTRODUCTION

With this block we return to the study of 'works of art' in the form of plays, music and fiction and we begin with one of the three literary genres: drama.

George Bernard Shaw's play *Pygmalion*, a not-too-serious mainstay of the British repertoire, was written in 1912, within a year of Alfred Russel Wallace's death. You would not be wasting your time if you compared how the two men anticipated social progress might be achieved.

The version of the play that Shaw authorized Penguin to print in 1941 is not what he wrote in 1912. It includes the additional scenes he wrote for Gabriel Pascal's film version of 1938. However, it isn't the film script either, since for that the text was massively cut and new lines and a more romantic ending which had been written by scriptwriters were added. Ideally, I would have preferred to study the original 1912 text, but that is not available at a reasonable price.

FIGURE 19.1  *Higgins meets Eliza. What do his gesture and her expression suggest? Henry Higgins (Leslie Howard) and Eliza (Wendy Hiller) in the film* Pygmalion *1938, produced by Gabriel Pascal, directed by Anthony Asquith. (The Raymond Mander and Joe Mitchenson Theatre Collection, Beckenham)*

We have recorded the play for you on audio-cassette (AC6 and AC7), following the 1941 version of the text but omitting the new scenes written for film. When you are listening you may, if you wish, follow the text simultaneously in the set book. At this stage I would prefer you just to listen if you can, partly because drama is for **performance** and reading it is an incomplete activity and partly because of the difference between the recorded play and the written text, just described. We deliberately chose a play that is not complicated by the dense poetic language that made scrutiny of the text so imperative in your study of the sonnet. In addition, you may know the story already because you've seen the play or film of *Pygmalion*, or of the musical *My Fair Lady*, which is derived from it. A fully staged version of any text for video was beyond our means, but for an audio production we were able to assemble a star-studded cast and hope you enjoy their performance.

## Dramatic conventions

### CASSETTES 6 AND 7

Listen to the play on AC6 and AC7 now. After listening, briefly jot down what you think are some of the main characteristics of plays, and how plays differ from other forms of literature. Don't be scared of mentioning the blatantly obvious.

### DISCUSSION

I'm sure you spotted that plays are composed of *dialogue* (people speaking, with the text divided into who says what) and are meant to be *performed*. They do not contain passages of narrative or descriptive text apart from stage directions.

---

But then things get more complicated. What does 'drama' mean? Has drama got to be dramatic? Let's go back to the beginning and think about **dialogue**. This is the technical term for the way in which the verbal content of a play is expressed as the words that the characters say to each other or the audience. We're going to look at this in more detail in relation to Act Two, but from the start it's important to grasp a basic element in dramatic **convention**. (A convention is a traditional practice which those who follow it consent to observe.) In a play a very high proportion of what is being communicated is delivered through what can be expressed in speech. Apart from what is spoken, everything else that the playwright wishes to express in combination with the producer, actors and designers must be done through body language, sound effects (including music) and the visible language of the staging. If you look at a page of a novel – *Wide Sargasso Sea* for instance – you will see that the proportions of speech to description are quite different. In choosing to write a play, the playwright has accepted certain limits, just as the poet who wants to write a sonnet agrees to abide by its conventions. You saw in Block 1 that the discipline of the sonnet form stimulates rather than hinders invention, and that this constitutes part of its appeal to the poet. Similarly, the constraints of drama stimulate invention: every problem is an opportunity. But the playwright needs more than verbal skills: 'wright' doesn't mean 'writer' but is derived from an Old English word for 'worker'. We're going to look at how *well-wrought* this play is.

At first glance it may appear that apart from the need to confine most of what he or she wants to say to what can be expressed in speech and gesture, there aren't many formal restrictions on the playwright. Nowadays you'd be right. (Modern poets have equally unlimited options too.) But in Western Europe from the Renaissance until the nineteenth century, formal conventions, derived from such models as the ancient 'classical' play of the kind you're going to study next (*Medea* by Euripides), were frequently advocated in the more élite or high-brow kinds of theatre. Elizabethan dramatists imitated the Roman philosopher Seneca in dividing their work into five acts. French Neoclassical court drama in the seventeenth century conformed to the three 'unities' that scholars perceived in the ancestral forms: that is, the action should restrict itself to a single **theme**, take place in one location, and occupy no longer than the events of a single day. Another convention was that significant and especially violent actions should take place off-stage: our word 'obscene' derives from a term meaning just that.

## EXERCISE

Can you detect any traces of these traditional rules in *Pygmalion*?

## DISCUSSION

You may have said that it restricts itself to a single theme, Eliza's transformation – although Alfred Doolittle is a bit of a digression – and I expect you noticed that it's divided into five acts. Yet you might well argue that it's divided into five episodes just because that's how many Shaw needed to tell his tale, and not because of any formal precedent. But turn to the set book and look for a moment at the lengthiest stretch of new material that Shaw inserted when the play was filmed in 1938 (pp.68–72), which forms a virtual sixth act. The ball is the climax of the story, and yet it takes place off-stage in the stage version. It would be extravagant and technically taxing to stage a ball within the confines of a theatre, and Shaw was very aware of the constraints as well as the opportunities of his chosen medium, but I think this absence also reveals his understanding of the essence of traditional conventions. A ball is hardly the prohibited 'violent' action of classical drama, but it distracts us from what Shaw believed to be the more important intellectual aspects of his play. If you have time, you could reread this episode to see if you agree with me that while you might imagine it would look very pretty, it doesn't add much to the argument. Indeed, if you see the film of *Pygmalion* or *My Fair Lady* ask yourself whether this highly decorative addition pushes the story towards the 'Cinderella' ending Shaw chose to avoid.

---

I don't mean that Shaw consciously said to himself 'I must observe the five-act divisions of the classical tradition', especially when Chekhov in Russia and Ibsen in Norway had already divided their work into just four acts, and in any case the English-speaking tradition had seldom been quite so formal. Shakespeare notoriously declined to observe the 'unities'. But the conventional five-act form allows the breakdown of action into five balanced sections: not just the *beginning, middle* and *end* which the Greek philosopher Aristotle sensibly defined as the essential stages in any good plot, but room for **development** (second act) before the middle or **climax** (third act), and a further complication or **turning-point** (fourth act) before the **denouement** or ending (fifth act). We shall be exploring these terms in relation to the five acts of Shaw's play, and in doing so I hope to show how his presentation of ideas (or what the play is 'about') is matched by his specific skills as a dramatist.

## Interpretation and context

I referred above to one difference between Shaw's stage and film versions of *Pygmalion*, and you have just listened to an audio recording. Any recorded performance is, of course, 'fixed' at the time of its making. TV19 (*A Living Doll: a background to Shaw's Pygmalion*) suggests ways in which Pascal's film is as much a product of its own time (1938) as of the period in which Shaw wrote the play. Even our recording will come to sound very dated. (It was made in 1996.) But in the theatre, 'live' performance is just that: *live*. What was started when the play was first put together is completed in the here and now when we see it performed in front of us. Even the most painstaking (or pedantic) reconstruction of how a play might originally have been performed happens *now*.

You saw in Block 3 how the spectator's historical viewpoint can influence his or her **interpretation** of a work of art. Thus, David's painting *Brutus* may appear to have been more explicitly motivated by the radical politics of its time than careful research reveals to have been the case. When we look at a painting as a reflection and comment on the circumstances in which it was produced this is not identical to the ways in which it was first viewed. This opens up a question which is of special interest where elements of performance are involved, but which occurs in the reception (the seeing, hearing or reading) of any work of art: *which matters most, the time of its origin or our response to it now?*

As this is such an important question for the whole course, pause and consider it now. ■

Some people have argued that the historical context doesn't matter and that a work of art can and should speak for itself. This is sometimes summed up in a phrase you may know: 'art for art's sake'. Others have contended that context is the sole key to understanding, and that the more we try to rid ourselves of our historical viewpoint and re-create that of the age in which the work was produced, the more will be revealed.

I expect you will have realized since Block 1 that although individual members of the course team hold different views, we all agree that the most rewarding position lies between these extremes. Most recently, in Unit 16, Jim Moore reminded us that 'everyone who studies the past is influenced by the present'. Learning about the historical context of a work helps to show what pressures contributed to form it, but it is only by being fully aware of our own context and perspective that we can get the most out of a work.

Live theatre brings together the 'then' of composition and the 'now' of performance in a way that many productions exploit when they highlight the relevance of a play's themes to the preoccupations of their own times. Thus, a 1980s, feminist production of *Pygmalion* might have suggested that Eliza Doolittle gets a raw deal, whilst *My Fair Lady* in the 1960s stressed the pretty frocks. On several occasions in this block we shall be introducing ideas about gender, race and culture which belong to our own age and which we cannot set aside just because the play we are watching is a century (or twenty centuries) old. We shall also see, later, that even where no actual performance takes place – as in reading a novel – the reader's response plays an active part in the formation of meaning.

# 2 ACT ONE

Now listen again to and/or reread Act One. Putting the audience in the picture at the beginning of a play is called **exposition**. (It *exposes* the starting-point.) The problem is to convey information, which the characters themselves may well know already, *within the limits of convincing dialogue*. I'm sure you've come across instances of how ludicrous this can sound when badly done.

Look at pp.18–19 where Henry Higgins and Colonel Pickering introduce themselves to each other and the audience. Then look back at what precedes this exchange and make lists of what we have learned about both characters beforehand.

You might well have noticed that until this point in the text the characters are only identified as 'the note taker' and 'the gentleman', respectively. Just as on the stage, if the play was new to you, you would not know who they were. You might indeed, like the bystanders, imagine that Higgins was a detective, 'taking … down' Eliza's words (p.13). Whatever his business, he has an uncanny ability to discover things he has not been told – that one bystander originated in Selsey, and that the mother comes from Epsom. This talent allows Shaw (via Higgins) to tell us all we need to know about Pickering's background in four words flat: 'Cheltenham, Harrow, Cambridge, and India' (p.15). Higgins himself is not so easily summed up. He is affable but overbearing, not downright cruel perhaps but surely insensitive. 'Bully' might not be too strong a word to use about him. And how he talks! It's completely plausible that such a self-announcing character would declare his profession, his abilities, his beliefs and his ambitions within a couple of pages of dialogue, as Higgins does on pages 17–18.

---

Whilst this is all in character, it's simultaneously a skilful part of the exposition, since it provides a synopsis of the elements already in place and a promise of what's going to happen: 'in three months I could pass that girl off as a duchess'. Not only does Eliza hear this, she also hears Higgins give Pickering his address. This is another perfectly credible scrap of dialogue but it isn't just there because it's **realistic**. It enables Eliza to turn up at Higgins's laboratory the next day without any cumbersome rigmarole about how a girl of her sort might have traced the whereabouts of a gentleman. Do you see how economical this is? Although I want to concentrate on stage-craft, I'd like to digress to look briefly at the interesting relationship between what is 'realistic' and theatrical illusion.

## Realism and illusion

We've already noticed that what seems convincingly life-like is none the less contrived. You might say there's more work in this work of art than meets the eye. First, however, a caution. I put 'realistic' in inverted commas to alert you to the complexity of this and related terms. '**Realism**' means 'a theory of the real'. (The suffix '-ism' always implies a theory.) As it is difficult enough to define what is real, it follows that theories that postulate any kind of relationship between the various arts and 'reality' are necessarily even more complex.

Not all drama is realistic. Pantomime, for example, is a familiar form of non-realist drama. But Shaw was writing at a time when three aspects of realism were converging in the London theatre. First, it was not uncommon in 1912 for the curtain to rise on an empty stage so that the elaborate, detailed and real-looking set might receive its own round of applause. *Pygmalion* calls for three such sets. This may help to remind you that realism, like scenery, is something *constructed*. Second, whilst many of the most popular Edwardian plays were frothy pieces of fairy-tale nonsense (as TV19 explains), 'realist' plays about serious moral issues were also being produced. John Galsworthy is a name you may know (he wrote *The Forsyte Saga*), and although his dramatic work is currently less regarded than that of his Norwegian contemporary Henrik Ibsen (author of *A Doll's House*, for example), whom Shaw himself championed on the London stage, both (like Shaw) were regarded as 'social realists'. Like the 'kitchen sink' drama of the 1950s and 1960s (such as *Look Back in Anger*), such work was often accused of being sordid. *Pygmalion*, however, which was Shaw's first big hit, cleverly managed to combine its elements of serious social realism with a rags-to-riches story. You may remember that in Study Week 1 Charles Harrison told us that the painter Courbet called himself a '"Realist", meaning that he aimed to show life as it was, not as it was supposed to be' (Unit 1, p.36). Well, although that doesn't say everything that might be said about the complicated business of representing life in terms of art, it's a good practical beginning.

The third 'realism' we can see in Shaw's plays is that of dialogue – that word again. With the partial exception of Higgins's characteristic grandiloquence, all the characters speak in recognizable everyday speech – stripped of its ums and ers, repetitions and tailings off, of course, but familiar none the less. It's difficult to appreciate now how momentous was the use of familiar language in the new plays of the late nineteenth century, because heightened, poetical language in drama was one of the most durable and pervasive legacies of the classical tradition. *Medea*, like all Greek tragedies, is in verse; a couple of thousand years later one of the arguments classically minded critics used against Shakespeare was that he sometimes wrote prose dialogue – a very unusual departure from the verse in which nearly all tragedy was written until well into the nineteenth century. Comedy, traditionally considered a less serious form, had generally been written in prose in Britain from the Restoration (1660) onwards. But until the second half of the nineteenth century nearly all serious drama in Europe had been written in verse: an elevated form of language befitting solemn themes.

During the nineteenth century, however, the realist novel became the most pervasive form of literature and new drama had to keep in step. When the set looked real, the plot concerned recognizable modern types and situations, and the language was comparable with the audience's own speech, it was possible to believe when the curtain rose that one was looking at an alternative slice of life. So powerful is this illusion that it's easy to think that this is the age-old norm of theatrical representation, whereas in the long, long history of the theatre it was actually a mere interlude. The Greeks did not wait for a curtain to disclose a brightly lit box, nor did Shakespeare's audience. You may have seen the reconstruction of the Globe Theatre on London's South Bank: no room for realistic sets there.

Yet even when drama does not aim to mimic the appearance, sound and behaviour of familiar life, performance and playing are inextricably associated with **imitation**. The speech that a playwright sets down and an actor performs can imitate 'real life' speech so closely that if you turn on your television at random you may not immediately know whether you're watching a drama or a documentary. Even when the words are not realistic, the emotion with which an actor performs them appeals to the audience's experience of similar emotions. It's unlikely that any young man in any age would exclaim 'O she doth teach the torches to burn bright!' as Romeo does when he first sets eyes on Juliet, but the emotion, the glow, the sudden lighting up of life are recognizably authentic. The actors who play these emotions are not marks on a page or canvas but men and women like ourselves. An essential part of the fascination of performance is that we feel it to be real at the same time as we know it is fake, rather as we can agree that a drawing of a shaded circle represents a sphere (see Unit 1, p.16). In both cases we make a tacit agreement to accept the illusion. Drama, however, is said to be the most 'mimetic' of the arts, a term that comes from the Greek word *mimesis* from which we also derive our words 'mime' and 'mimicry'. In drama, imitation embodies, brings to life, enacts the story in materials (actors, props, settings) that are often identical and always physically comparable to what is being represented.

Now, I'm not trying to claim any superior characteristics for drama as a form of art. Indeed, imitation as such tends to be looked down on, and in many cultures dramatic imitation or impersonation has been regarded with suspicion or contempt because it blurs the distinction between the authentic and the stand-in. (This argument originates in Plato's *Republic*, Book III, and the opponents of Tudor and Jacobean playhouses later objected that if an actor played a king, might he not get ideas above his station? We still argue about confusion between real and simulated violence, and its possible consequences.) We must also remember that 'performance' elides the skills of two different but mutually dependent entities: the playwright and the actor. You could compare the composer and the instrumentalist in music, but in drama the actor is also the instrument. To see how incomplete a play is without performances, think of a song without the singer. Performance is literally *essential* to drama – of its essence or being. A play will only be good *as a play* if it performs well, and so the most effective playwrights are those who best understand performance and the theatre.

# Stage-craft

We have already seen how skilfully and economically Shaw unwraps and explains his characters – and thus we return from our digression to Shaw's stage-craft. Even though his approach is broadly 'realistic', truth to life isn't necessarily his reason for doing something.

## EXERCISE

Reread or listen again to the play until the entrance of 'the gentleman' (Pickering): 'Phew!' Why did Shaw open his play as he did?

(Let me give you a practical tip. If the work you are studying is of any stature, then every word, every note, every brushstroke contributes something. Vacuity, hot air or pointless repetition are not likely to be much of a feature in any artefact selected for study (unless the point of that study is to help you identify such things), and so you can assume that when you're asked a question like this the answer will not be 'Because he couldn't think of anything better'.)

## DISCUSSION

Yet you might well have felt that Shaw couldn't think of anything better here, because all the 'to-do' about a cab seems so very inconsequential. Then imagine what the audience is doing at this point: coughing, letting late-comers through, shushing and settling down. It would be a foolish writer who attempted to convey any essential information in the first minute after curtain-up. Then think about the cab. When does Freddy finally manage to find one? Too late, of course, which is only to be expected of nice-but-dim characters like Freddy; but just in time for Eliza to sweep off triumphantly. So the cab he was sent to find at the beginning neatly wraps up the end of the act. At the beginning of the act Freddy bumps into Eliza and upsets her flower basket; at its end he encounters her again. It's nicely symmetrical, and of course their paths are going to cross again in Act Three.

---

There's more to be said about Act One, but before then, look briefly at the very beginning and the end of each of the other four acts. (The stage ending of Act Four is Eliza tearing off her ring. The episode with Freddy was added for the more romantic demands of the film.) You'll see that Acts Two and Three also begin and end symmetrically, which underlines our sense that although a lot happens in each act, it is contained and under control. But Act Four is quite different. It ends angrily, violently and unsymmetrically because what has happened (Eliza's revolt) cannot be contained. This is the 'turning-point' and things are not as they were. The ending of the last act is discussed in TV19 and we shall return to it later. I hope you will agree that, although unobtrusive, these structural details are methodical and effective.

FIGURE 19.2   *Compare this moment from the original production with the still from the 1938 film shown in Figure 19.1. Which suggests a more equal relationship between Eliza and Higgins? Eliza (Mrs Patrick Campbell), Henry Higgins (Sir Herbert Tree) in 1914 production of* Pygmalion, *His Majesty's Theatre, London. (The Raymond Mander and Joe Mitchenson Theatre Collection, Beckenham)*

We've considered the opening act of the play in terms of its construction, or how the pieces of the story are arranged, but what does it add to what the play's about? Break this down a bit. What do the mother, daughter and Freddy (the Eynsford-Hills) stand for?

## EXERCISE

I called Freddy 'nice-but-dim'. Can you sum up his mother and sister in a phrase or two? Think about what they are doing, what happens to them and how they react. I haven't drawn attention to their actual words because I want you to fill out our recording and imagine you are seeing it in a theatre.

## DISCUSSION

On stage or screen their clothes, faces and body language would reinforce what in a sound-only recording their voices convey. They are middle-class, veering on 'posh', in a play that is going to be about class, and middle-class gentility and morality in particular.

A high proportion of Shaw's original audience (and a fair proportion of today's) would have come from just that class, which is likely to assume that its attitudes are the norm from which everyone else deviates. What establishes that these specimens are to be laughed at, rather than with, is that they are so very helpless. 'We must have a cab' wails Mrs Eynsford-Hill plaintively, as if her wish were heaven's command. But she is marginally more sympathetic than her daughter, whose response to her situation seem quite disproportionate.

## EXERCISE

Clara reacts almost hysterically to Higgins's civil question about a cab: 'Dont dare speak to me' (p.16). Can you think why the part is written like this?

## DISCUSSION

If the actress plays that out-of-proportion note for all its worth (instead of just sliding over it trying to sound reasonably convincing) then what comes across is Clara's anxiety about being out late at night amongst the disreputable classes.

## EXERCISE

Look at the passage where Mrs Eynsford-Hill buys a bunch of Eliza's flowers. What thoughts or feelings might prompt Clara to say 'you might have spared Freddy that'?

## DISCUSSION

This is not just meanness (although we learn later that the Eynsford-Hills are hard up: none are so anxious about their status as those in most danger of losing it), nor does it stem from a conviction that she's bound to be cheated. It's her mother's direct question that embarrasses Clara: 'Now tell me how *you* know that young *gentleman's* name.' I've added italics to show you how Mrs Eynsford-Hill's words highlight the unthinkable possibility that her son might be personally 'known' to this class of person. (Eliza doesn't know Freddy. She calls him 'Freddy' much as a stage Glaswegian might call any stranger 'Jimmeh'.)

Although these are only minor characters they play an important role in providing parallels or mirrors to the main characters. In Act Three, Clara, like Freddy, will be quite bowled over by the new lady-like Eliza, although their mother, who half recognizes her, still has her misgivings. Once again, Eliza will sweep off in a taxi, leaving Freddy gaping behind her. Clara can't wait to try Eliza's small talk at her next tea-party: in an unemphatic way they are sisters under the skin. Just as in Act Three Clara needs social affirmation as much as (and far more frantically than) Eliza, so in Act One she's equally nervous (although with less good reason) about her social status being mistaken for something less than respectable. Not only do situations echo each other and pull the fabric of the play into a satisfactorily tight pattern; characters also mirror each other, and the reflections shed light on the parts concerned.

# 3 ACT TWO

In a conventional five-act play, the second act is concerned with development.

## EXERCISE

Now listen again to and/or reread Act Two. In what ways does this part of the play develop or build on the exposition that has taken place in Act One?

## DISCUSSION

It's not until we get to the end of Act Two that we can see how complete was the exposition in Act One. Of course, this is hardly the kind of response you're likely to make to your companion in the next seat at the theatre, but it is part of the unobtrusive skill of the good playwright that makes the play very satisfying – or so I hope you're finding it. Although it is neither dull nor predictable, Act Two contains no very great surprises and everything follows on from the premises sketched in Act One.

Perhaps the philosophical term 'premises' surprised you, but it is quite often used metaphorically of drama to refer to those 'statements' from which the conclusion must follow. 'Statements' is in scare-quotes here because dramatic premises are usually more elusive than those in a simple syllogism. But the comparison is illuminating because the exposition effectively supplies us with the given propositions from which the conclusion will eventually seem to follow with inescapable logic.

The given propositions are that on the one hand we have a spirited and socially aspirational flower girl, and on the other a pair of toffs professionally equipped to pass her off as a duchess. Eliza has taken on board what she learned the previous night and decided that there is a good opportunity here. We don't see her working this out because it's all so obvious. Act Two brings together the coinciding ambitions of the characters and raises and elaborates on at least some of the problems inherent in the situation.

## Stage-business

As I suggested earlier, in art as in life every problem can be an opportunity. Let's look at how getting Eliza out of her old clothes and beginning her transformation provides opportunities for *stage-business* – effects achieved not by words, or not by words alone. First, Shaw endows his characters with a bottomless purse and a magically swift department store delivery service. The Japanese dress that Eliza wears after her bath is the only item of female clothing that a confirmed bachelor might plausibly be expected to possess, because a contemporary vogue for all things Japanese had lead to a fashion for displaying kimonos as part of one's home furnishings. But there's also plenty of opportunity for comic business here. Look for another example at the episode involving Eliza's presumably flea-ridden hat (p.50). In both instances you can see that the words form only a tiny part of what will be going on at this point in the performance.

Now let's consider how different media can present different problems and opportunities.

### EXERCISE

First read from the middle of page 34, 'Bundle her off to the bathroom', to the bottom of page 52, 'I cant account for it', *leaving out* the section between the asterisks (* * *), which was written for the film. Then read the section between the asterisks on its own. What can this section do that theatre cannot, and what, if anything, is lost?

### DISCUSSION

The scene written for the cinema is too technically complicated for a stage setting, and it permits titillating suggestions of nudity too risky to be stage-managed in front of an Edwardian audience. But Shaw also takes the opportunity to tell his audience that Eliza thinks cleanliness is unnatural because being clean takes money, privacy and warmth. Her prudishness is comically perverse. After all, it's the well-to-do who are supposed to be more 'proper', as we shall be reminded in Act Five by the newly gentrified Alfred Doolittle's disquisition on 'middle class morality'.

I don't feel altogether comfortable with the stripping and forcible bathing of Eliza: we'll return to the strain of violence in the play later. (If your reaction was 'Things were different then', think of the imprisonment and force-feeding of the suffragettes, part of the 'background' referred to in TV19.) You may also have found the scene patronizing. I think it diverts attention from the amusing paradox in the dialogue on pages 39–40 which helps fill the time in the theatre production while the actress is changing off-stage. Mrs Pearce establishes that the professor and the flower girl are equally given to bad language, but who really has the most disgusting and unhygienic habits?

---

Both Eliza's reaction to undressing and washing and Higgins's undomesticated habits exhibit just the kind of paradox that Shaw delighted in. The phrase 'Shavian paradox' is sometimes used to describe a delight in turning all kinds of truisms and commonplaces upside down. Doolittle, who now strides incongruously onto the scene, is the embodiment of further Shavian paradoxes, and he too is an opportunity created out of a problem. It's Mrs Pearce who asks the sensible question 'Where's your mother?' (p.31). As a single woman, of independent though slender means, Eliza needs explaining. In real life, plenty of women lived alone and earned their own living. The 1901 census recorded 5.3 million women wage-earners and in 1911 there were 1068 women in the population for every 1000 males. Nevertheless, on stage the single working-class woman *who was not a victim* was apparently so implausible that she needed to be accounted for. It's amazing how many heroines in fiction are motherless – far more than was ever realistic – but if they had had good mothers to guide and protect them, they wouldn't have had any adventures. Shaw could have solved the problem of Eliza's family by killing off her father as well, but as Lady Bracknell says in a slightly older play (which Shaw disliked): 'To lose one parent ... may be regarded as a misfortune; to lose both looks like carelessness' (Oscar Wilde, *The Importance of Being Earnest*, 1895). Wilde was making fun of the absence of fictional mothers that I've just referred to.

Besides, Shaw has another problem. Eliza has been packed off-stage to be scrubbed up, and how is he to fill the interval? First, he reflects on Higgins's personal uncleanliness, then introduces an even more unwashed character, the stereotypical cockney dustman – who turns out not to be stereotypical at all. Thematically, Doolittle allows Shaw to ponder the question of whether social advancement is always a benefit. When, in Act Five, he becomes a prey to the middle-class morality he could not earlier afford, his comic discomfort about what is to become of him parallels the unease about what is to become of his daughter.

Doolittle eventually runs rings round Higgins, leaving the audience with a pleasing sense that the Professor and the Colonel are not going to have everything their own way. But let's look at the successive stages of the encounter and try to identify what's 'dramatic' about it. On stage (or on film, of course) Doolittle's very appearance is dramatic because he forms such a striking contrast to the other characters. It's worth remembering that our most casual uses of the word 'dramatic' (as in 'That's a dramatic sunset', for example) frequently imply a sense of strong contrasts. Here, we're certainly presented with a stage-picture that contains an extreme

FIGURE 19.3   *What do the hand gestures of the three characters each suggest here? Notice that Eliza is wearing her old hat with the Professor's kimono. What kind of stage-business might this allow? Eliza (Mrs Patrick Campbell), Alfred Doolittle (Edmund Gurney) and Henry Higgins (Sir Herbert Tree) in 1914 production of* Pygmalion, His Majesty's *Theatre, London. (The Raymond Mander and Joe Mitchenson Theatre Collection, Beckenham)*

social contrast. But how does this notion of dramatic 'contrast' apply to the dialogue? It's very rich here and at first glance may not seem to depend quite as much on non-verbal elements of performance as did the interaction in connection with Eliza's hat, where Mrs Pearce's gingerly handling of the offending object and Higgins's startled reaction will convey far more than their words alone.

## Looking at dialogue

**EXERCISE**

Think of the dialogue as a fight and go through it marking each speech as if it produces a gain (+) or loss (-) for its speaker. Try also to identify the points where the tide of battle turns. I doubt if we'll agree about every plus and minus. The point of the exercise is to bring out the dynamics of the dialogue.

## DISCUSSION

Doolittle starts with a direct attack ('a very serious matter': p.41), is temporarily deflated by Higgins's apparently irrelevant response but comes back even stronger: 'I want my daughter'. Higgins disarms him by seeming to agree and then presses his advantage with a series of attacking moves: 'How dare you come here?' (p.42). But then he makes an unforced error – 'This is ... a plot' – which gives his adversary a renewed opening: 'Have I asked you for a brass farthing?' In a flash, Doolittle regains the point he has just conceded ('Well, what would a man come for?') and Higgins in turn is 'disarmed'.

Even in a reading, you can detect these rhythms. In performance, you can hear how the varying pace, volume and emphasis of the speeches underline the to-and-fro of the argument. In a staged performance movement (sitting, standing; advance or retreat) and body language would all contribute to the effect.

At this point the pace changes to supply the explanation for Doolittle's arrival on the scene, and if you look at the comparative length and leisureliness of Doolittle's speeches (p.43) I think you'll see that he's now perfectly at ease. Then Pickering wrong-foots himself and Doolittle is given the opportunity for another of his rhetorical questions: 'Have I said a word about taking her away?' By now he's asking questions that are grandly self-righteous and questions that are downright immoral in very similar forms and tones. So adroit are his argumentative postures that he gradually sounds quite reasonable: 'Heres a career opening for her as you might say'.

With Mrs Pearce's entrance, reinforcements arrive. Part of the joke, of course, is that neither man has any intention that Eliza should leave, and so when Mrs Pearce says that when her clothes arrive there will be nothing to stop her, the adversaries are forced into an alliance (of 'men of the world') which banishes Mrs Pearce from the male improprieties which she fears are about to be exchanged. But in sending her away, Higgins has made a dangerous concession, and from now on the floor is Doolittle's, while Higgins for once admits that he doesn't know what to do (p.45). He and Pickering (gentlemen and scholars both) are helplessly unable to challenge the argument that a poor man should sell his daughter for a fiver to spend on a bender. So much for the middle-class morality which keeps the 'undeserving' Doolittle poor. So tickled is Higgins by this chop-logic that he is prepared to pay twice as much as the dustman has asked for – an offer which Doolittle loftily declines. By the middle of page 47 the moral high-ground is the dustman's alone: what middle-class morality would call fecklessness (at least) is construed as 'giving pleasure ... employment ... and satisfaction'; and even fornication (which Pickering 'rather draw[s] the line at encouraging') is rendered topsy-turvily as obligation ('I got to be agreeable to her') rather than as libertine indulgence – which is how censorious middle-class morality would regard it. He crowns this with advice so smugly misogynistic (p.47) as to be *almost* beyond offence.

---

Doolittle's departure at this point (pp.47–48) would be an anti-climax, but this is prevented by the reappearance of a now unrecognizable Eliza. This is very clearly a highly 'dramatic' moment in that it obviously depends much less on words than on performance and theatrical presentation for its impact. Yet if you glance back at the scene we have just studied, you'll see that there too, although the verbal content is very rich, the full impact is waiting to be realized through performance.

If you skim the whole of this act – or indeed the whole play – I think you'll agree that a very large proportion of the dialogue consists of argument, altercation, disagreement or cross-purposes – probably a much higher proportion than most of us could cope with in 'real life'. Without at least a little of the heat that friction generates, conversation is seldom 'dramatic' – that is to say, it does not possess the qualities that make it a potentially interesting spectacle. So it is the business of the dramatist to find ways of expressing his or her chosen themes through characters whose words and postures will interact most vividly. You could think of the dramatic impulse as that which *maximizes the contrasts in any given situation*. If Doolittle knew that Higgins had no 'designs' on his daughter, understood that elocution lessons would give her a start in life, and came to a sensible agreement about how the domestic arrangements were to be kept respectable, this might be more realistic, but it would be deadly dull.

# 4 ACT THREE

Now listen again to and/or reread Act Three. This act is the *climax*, which turns out not to be the climax at all, because unexpectedly the play's business is shown to be incomplete (see page 12 above). I'm reminding you that in its division of the action, *Pygmalion* conforms to traditional patterns. Indeed, **tradition** is going to be the main theme of your work on this act, although I want to approach it somewhat indirectly. Even though Act Three turns out to be something of an anti-climax, it is the high point of the play, in that this is the funniest and indeed most spectacular scene. (Remember that the stage version of the play did not include the ball.)

### EXERCISE

Think for a moment about what I have just said about drama's *maximization of contrasts*, and identify what is the most striking contrast in this scene.

## DISCUSSION

Eliza now looks and sounds (as far as register and accent go) totally transformed. But her appearance and manners are in utter contrast to the unreconstructed *matter* of her conversation, which is entirely incongruous in a polite drawing room. This is the main contrast, but you may have noticed others such as the contrast between Eliza and Clara. Whilst the former is trying to move up the social scale by imitating 'nice' manners, the other imagines she can become fashionable by aping a 'lower' class idiom.

FIGURE 19.4   *A positively dashing spectacle: in a new scene added to the musical* My Fair Lady, *Eliza shocks the staid Ascot racegoers by encouraging her horse to move his 'bloomin' 'arse'. Why do you think the 1938 film and the musical added spectacular new scenes such as the ball scene and this scene at Ascot? Eliza (Audrey Hepburn), Henry Higgins (Rex Harrison) and Colonel Pickering (Wilfred Hyde White) in the Ascot scene from the film* My Fair Lady *1964, Warner Brothers. (Reproduced by courtesy of the Kobal Collection)*

When the act opens, Higgins and Pickering are convinced that they are close to success. I want now to look in some detail at why the play can't end here. Turn once again to the passage that starts on page 64 when Mrs Higgins tells her 'silly boy' that of course Eliza is not 'presentable' – a word that had a literal meaning when debutantes were still 'presented' at court.

## EXERCISE

What is Mrs Higgins most concerned about?

## DISCUSSION

She is not worried about how many more lessons Eliza will need before she can pass muster. This is all the crestfallen Pickering seems to consider when he talks about 'something to eliminate the sanguinary element'. But in the teeth of the men's short-sighted enthusiasms, Mrs Higgins urges the larger question of 'what is to be done with her afterwards' (p.67). This is not unlike Mrs Pearce's repeated question in Act Two: 'what is to become of her?'

*Both women have a better understanding than the main characters of what is taking place and they ask searching questions about it.* I emphasize this because it is another example of a feature that appears quite 'realistic' but has its roots in ancient traditions.

## Myths and tradition

In Greek tragedy a chorus of onlookers is often used to express 'a better understanding than the main characters ... and ... ask searching questions'. The chorus represents something like the audience's most alert and challenging response, and formally integrates a commentary on the action within it. Thus, when you study *Medea* in the coming weeks, you'll see that, incongruous though any comparison between this drawing-room comedy and one of the most horrifying of Greek tragedies might seem to be, nevertheless Mrs Pearce and Mrs Higgins could be described as 'choric', in that, like a Greek chorus, they form a kind of on-stage audience, asking on our behalf the questions that the dramatist wants us to consider.

You'll have to wait until next week before deciding whether you're convinced by this comparison, and I cannot try to add more weight to my argument by claiming that Shaw was deliberately copying classical forms because I do not know of any such evidence. But as an experienced dramatist and drama critic, Shaw was steeped in dramatic tradition, and many forms and conventions had become second nature to him. In Block 1 you saw how the sonnet form handed on and developed a tradition that became almost like the lineage of a family tree. The European dramatic tradition is even older and more diverse, and yet features of the remotest ancestors can still sometimes be detected in their most recent descendants. What is a relatively modern emphasis on originality (and/or novelty) has tended to devalue the role and function of artistic traditions, but each successive generation of artistic production (in whatever form) builds on what has preceded it – even when it reacts most strongly against what has gone before.

We have already had occasion to notice several ways in which the quite unobtrusive form of *Pygmalion* resembles its dramatic ancestors. In Block 1, however, you saw that it was not just the sonnet *form* that was handed on from generation to generation of poets: there has been a continuity in the content too. So Seamus Heaney can draw on all the accumulated love that the form has recorded when he remembers so tenderly his mother peeling potatoes (Unit 2, p.55).

## EXERCISE

What aspects of *Pygmalion*'s content, story or theme do you think might relate in some way to traditional stories?

## DISCUSSION

You might recall phrases like 'rags to riches' (page 15 above) or even 'Cinderella' (page 12 above) and think that these are applicable. But the other clue to this play's ancestral story has been staring at you every time you picked it up: the title, *Pygmalion*.

It's strange how often we fail to register the significance of a title, so you might well have missed this or not even thought about what it refers to if you don't know the Greek myth about Pygmalion. (On the other hand, you were advised in your first week's work to consider the titles of paintings, so if you've transferred the lesson, be pleased with yourself.)

Before we look at the story of Pygmalion as it was told by the Roman poet Ovid, during the reign of the Emperor Augustus, just before the beginning of the Common Era, consider for a moment the word 'myth', emphasized in the title of this block. You may have wondered when you would meet it. Like many words with 'y' and 'th' or 'ph' in them, it derives from a Greek word – in this case *mythos* – and indeed it is to the unlikely legends of Greek (and Roman) gods and heroes (and goddesses and heroines) that we commonly attach the word. The *Oxford English Dictionary* (OED) defines 'myth' as:

> A purely fictitious narrative usually involving supernatural persons, actions or events, and embodying some popular idea concerning natural or historical phenomena.

This is very different from Arthur Marwick's use of the word in TV8, where he implied 'a story widely believed to be true but which turns out to be not completely true or even invented'. As he says at the beginning of Unit 8, many of the really important words we use have several meanings. For sure, both meanings here imply that myths are fictitious, even though we might object to the OED's 'purely' because a myth may have a distant grounding in some actual or historical event. Whether or not there is any factual 'truth' in a myth has no bearing on the *value* we may attach to it.

There is an element of acquired value that is crucial to all myths, ancient and modern. Frequently this can be expressed as a warning that our mistakes or wrong-doing will catch up with us: the story of Don Juan (you will meet this in Week 22) is such a myth, and so I think are many modern 'urban myths'. Myths are stories that express some kind of generalized lesson, and as they are usually quite simple stories they are capable of considerable variations, in which although the incidentals change the core of significance remains much the same. Perhaps because they can be and so often are retold, the origins of myths are frequently obscure. Our concern in this block is to demonstrate that just as artistic forms have a history, so does the narrative content of those genres in literature, painting and music that tell a story. Artists of all kinds have dipped into the bottomless myth-kitty for stories that can be relevantly reworked yet retain their universal application.

If you are new to the study of some or all of the arts, it isn't easy to appreciate the importance of tradition, because you simply don't know a wide enough range of examples to be able to trace these family likenesses. If you continue you'll gradually acquire a sufficient body of knowledge; we were all in the same boat once. Myths are only one of the ways in which the arts replenish themselves by building on what has gone before, but they provide a relatively accessible way of illustrating this principle because they are to some extent a feature of generalized rather than specialized knowledge. The Pygmalion myth may not be as familiar as the story of Cinderella, but I doubt whether this will be the first time you've come across the idea of a body assembled by an artist or scientist which comes to life.

I now want to consider an extract from Ovid's *Metamorphoses*. This collection of myths is one of art's most prolific ancestors, the source or inspiration for countless works of literature, painting and sculpture. As the tales were already familiar when Ovid compiled them, they were not, of course, invented by him, but he did assemble a diverse mass of ancient material in a narrative that purported to account for the origins of the Roman Empire from the world's original 'metamorphosis' (or 'transformation' as it might be translated) out of chaos. Many of the stories themselves concern individual 'transformations' – as does the tale of Pygmalion's statue. (Other famous metamorphoses include the disguises assumed by Jupiter, chief of the gods, in his pursuit of mortal women.) Again, I do not know whether Shaw actually looked up the story of Pygmalion in Ovid's *Metamorphoses*, but it was popular among artists and poets in the late nineteenth century and the gist of it was commonplace.

340 P.OVIDII METAMOR-    P.OVID'S METAMOR-
F A B. IX. *Pygmalion in Love with a Statue.*

### *THE ARGUMENT.*

Pygmalion a famous Statuary, provoked by the diſſolute Lives of the Propœtides, throws off all Fondneſs of the Sex, and reſolves on a perpetual Celibacy. He afterwards falls in Love with a Statue he had made. Venus, at his Requeſt, animates it; he marries his newly inſpired Miſtreſs, and has a Son by her, who built the City of Paphos, which bears the Name of its Founder.

FIGURE 19.5 *Does Shaw's Higgins adore his creation as Pygmalion loves his statue? Pygmalion in Love with a Statue, from Ovid,* Metamorphoses, *translated by Sir Samuel Garth, 1717, Amsterdam, p.340. (Bodleian Library, University of Oxford, 29816.b.1)*

## EXERCISE

Read Ovid's 'Pygmalion in Love with a Statue' in *Resource Book 3* (C1) and respond to the following questions. (Note: if you have already watched TV19, you will be familiar with some of the issues raised in these questions.) The translation is by Sir Samuel Garth. It dates from 1717 and the verse conveys something of Ovid's reputation for light-hearted eroticism.

1   Why do you think this particular myth might appeal to artists?

2   What equivalent stage in Ovid's story have we reached in Act Three of Shaw's play?

3   What is the most important difference between Shaw's version of the story and Ovid's?

## DISCUSSION

1   The artist would be especially well placed to identify with and explore the relation between creator and creation.

2   You could say that in Act Three Higgins (like the milder-mannered Pickering) is besotted with his creation. Skim the scene again to see if you agree. Mrs Higgins provides a significant clue when she describes them as 'a pretty pair of babies, playing with your live doll' (p.65) – although the word 'live' is a bit misleading because at this stage Eliza is behaving like some elaborately programmed automaton, more like a statue than a living woman. But at this point the replay of the myth is only half-complete. Making a beautiful statue is not enough, in particular for an artist with a social and educative mission like Shaw, who always despised merely frivolous or decorative art.

3   The endings of the stories are notably different. Unlike Pygmalion, Higgins does not fall in love with his creation, although, as TV19 explains, the play has frequently been given a romantic reading.

Myths, legends and familiar tales tend to be retold only when the re-teller sees in them something of relevance to his or her own times or condition. Thus, in recent years – for example – many fairy-tales have been retold from a feminist point of view. What attracted Shaw to the Ovidian myth was not any particular relevance to themes of social mobility, but more its concern with the role and powers of the artist and the autonomy and rights of the 'statue'. Higgins, like Pygmalion, has no time for women and Eliza is Higgins's equivalent of Pygmalion's statue. She is in a sense his creation. At the same time she is Shaw's creation too. He – with a little help from an actress – brings her to life.

(This thought may make you wonder whether Higgins is a self-portrait of his author. At this point you could read (quite quickly) the Preface to the play, which suggests a comparison between Higgins and the irascible phonetician Henry Sweet, who is referred to in TV19. Although Shaw says that Higgins has 'touches of Sweet', I still think Higgins sounds like Shaw's mouthpiece, if only because we never have any sense that Shaw disagrees with or disapproves of even Higgins's worst behaviour. He is a very indulged character and he always has the last word: two infallible indicators of favouritism. Shaw's plays are full of characters like Higgins – bossy, over-bearing, aggressive pedagogues who as teacher or mentor are in some sense the creator of the pupils they shape.)

I expect that you realized that Shaw rejected any romantic ending to the story because he wanted to avoid a conventional conclusion. If you remembered the 'Shavian paradoxes' of Doolittle's arguments, you might have thought he did it out of a characteristic desire to be awkward or perverse, and I think you'd be right. Shaw hated to be predictable. TV19 suggests some of the other psychological reasons why Shaw might have withheld the gratification of a 'wedding-bells' ending. There will be more to say about how the play ends when we get there.

# 5  ACTS FOUR AND FIVE

Now listen again to and/or reread Acts Four and Five consecutively. This is not just because Act Four is so short, but to get a better sense of how the pace and tone of the play change in its second half. Then, in order to give you a change of voice, turn to Lisë Pedersen's article, 'Shakespeare's *The Taming of the Shrew* vs. Shaw's *Pygmalion*: Male Chauvinism vs. Women's Lib?' (reprinted from *Fabian Feminist: Bernard Shaw and Woman*, ed. R. Weintraub), in *Resource Book 3* (C2).

## A look at a scholarly article

As this is the first time you have been asked to read a scholarly article on a literary topic, it's worth considering a few points before you embark.

**EXERCISE**

First, what can you deduce from the title of the article and its source? What you learned in Units 8 and 9 will be useful here.

**DISCUSSION**

Even if you didn't have the publication date, a couple of other clues might have suggested that this article may be old-fashioned. 'Women's Lib' is a seriously dated phrase and 'woman' – meaning some essential common denominator of all women – is again not much used now. Like the texts it deals with, a scholarly article is a product of the time and circumstances in which it was written. We have not had room to devote much attention to Shaw's personal politics, and so the term 'Fabian' (which refers to the non-revolutionary socialist group founded at the end of the nineteenth century) may have puzzled you in this connection, although it is referred to in TV19. 'Feminist', on the other hand, will be a more familiar term, but you may have wondered whether it could be properly applied to Shaw. The article itself will help you to make up your mind about that. Finally, you may have anticipated with some unease that the article will expect you to know a play that you possibly haven't seen or read.

---

You need not worry about this. For one thing, this is a problem that scholars never quite grow out of, because although it does diminish the more we read, no-one has ever read everything (although they may pretend to have done so). We learn to acquire knowledge where we can, and live with the limits of our reading, whilst seizing every opportunity to expand our range. In addition, although you may not have read Shakespeare's play *The Taming of the Shrew*, you've probably heard of both him and it, and perhaps you've seen the film, or the musical *Kiss Me Kate* which is based on it, or the film of the musical. It's a play that has had almost as varied an afterlife as *Pygmalion*. The title is virtually proverbial, and I'm sure you'll recognize that taming wild women is the theme of countless myths, so I think you'll know all you need to know about it.

## EXERCISE

In order to give you a little practice in the kind of effective reading that will stand you in good stead in more than just the present circumstances, as you read try to answer the following questions by identifying (perhaps highlighting) the phrases or sentences in the article that supply the information. Don't cheat! You'll feel the benefit later. Now read the article.

1  What convinces Pedersen that some elements in 'Shaw's depiction' were suggested by Shakespeare's play?

2  What did Shaw believe his own play achieved, but *The Taming of the Shrew* did not?

3  What does Pedersen identify as the primary similarity between the two plays?

4  What does Pedersen identify as the one challenge to Higgins's bullying?

5  What evidence is there that Shaw knew Shakespeare's play and what did he think of it?

6   How does Pedersen describe Eliza's original character in Shaw's play and do you agree with her assessment?

7   (More difficult!) How does Shaw's play repudiate traditional expressions of male dominance?

8   Does *Pygmalion* 'reject the concept of male dominance over women'?

## DISCUSSION

1   'Shaw deals with fictitious characters who, though bearing different names and occurring in different ages, are nevertheless in themselves or their situations so similar to characters and situations depicted by Shakespeare that it is difficult to believe that Shaw's depiction was not, whether consciously or unconsciously so, suggested by Shakespeare's.'

2   The implication must be that Shaw (unlike the bard) did 'force the public to reconsider its morals' and we've seen mischievous examples of this principle in action in the character of Doolittle. Remember this phrase, because we'll return to it later.

[Did you notice incidentally that Pedersen does not give a source for this quotation? Shaw actually says something like this quite frequently. At the end of *The Quintessence of Ibsenism* he says: 'We want a frankly doctrinal theatre' (Holroyd, 1986, p.175). If you wanted in an essay to exemplify Shaw's call for morally didactic drama, you could quote that sentence. Ideally, you would look it up to make sure I've got it right and that I haven't distorted his meaning by quoting out of context, but you couldn't look up Pedersen's quotation. It's every bit as important to be able to establish the provenance of your evidence in a literary debate as it is in an historical essay.]

3   'In both plays a man accepts the task of transforming a woman.'

4   Pickering's line 'Does it occur to you, Higgins, that the girl has some feelings?' This line is later echoed by Eliza herself.

5   A pseudonymous letter and an article are cited, which establish Shaw's very negative opinion of the character of the shrew-tamer Petruchio and the degradation suffered by Kate. Although the attitudes depicted might have been acceptable to Shakespeare's contemporaries, Shaw believes they are 'disgusting to modern sensibility'.

6   'Eliza ... was completely lacking in self-control, very quick to take offense, and very bad-tempered' – all of which needed the transforming influences of Pickering. This seems a bit harsh to me. As a young, single working woman, Eliza needs to be quick in her own defence. Perhaps this is another instance where Pedersen's reaction is a little dated; she would seem to have preferred a more docile Eliza.

7   Eliza explains to Pickering that she could not have learned to be a 'lady' from Higgins's uncouth example and that she gained the beginning of 'self-respect' from Pickering's use of her formal name. Higgins, as his sixteenth-century counterpart does with 'Kate', abuses Eliza's name. Although (with one exception, which Pedersen perhaps takes too lightly) physical abuse is repudiated, Higgins subjects Eliza to plenty of verbal abuse, but that is ultimately ineffective. In other words, it is Pickering not Higgins whose methods are really effective in the transformation. The argument goes that Shaw, unlike Shakespeare, is opposed to coercive methods of educating or reforming women because kinder methods prevail, whilst violence 'is an admission of defeat'.

8   Pedersen claims that both Eliza and Higgins reject it (and she supports her argument with quotes) so it's probably fair to say that in some respects the play as a whole endorses this view. Certainly, there's no counter-argument within it. Doolittle, who once advised Higgins to take a strap to Eliza, is a subdued character by the end. But are you completely convinced? After all, Higgins does claim the credit for 'making a woman' of Eliza and I do not see much sign that he regrets or intends to reform his domineering attitude.

---

There are several points in this which we shall return to, but first we should continue with our more general work on dramatic conventions.

## EXERCISE

Earlier (page 17 above) I suggested that Act Four traditionally contains a '*turning-point*'. Can you identify this?

## DISCUSSION

You might well have said that in Act Four 'the worm turns'. Eliza is fed up with having her hard work and feelings ignored. Higgins has treated her as an experiment, not a person, and so although he may think his bet is safely won and the story has ended, it's not all over for Eliza. Her question, 'What's to become of me?' (p.76), is still to be answered.

---

You'll be aware now that the triumphant ball scene conclusion we might have expected isn't *staged* at all because Shaw, who relished dramatic argument above theatrical spectacle, wanted to follow through other issues in the play. In *The Quintessence of Ibsenism* he argued that 'discussion' has taken the place of 'unravelling' in the latter stages of a serious modern play (Holroyd, 1986, p.160). Let's look more closely at the themes of the 'discussion' in this case.

FIGURE 19.6   *Does the addition of a decorative scene like this tempt its audience to think more in terms of the Cinderella story? Eliza (Audrey Hepburn), Colonel Pickering (Wilfred Hyde White) and Queen of Transylvania (Verocia Rothschild) in the ball scene, from the film My Fair Lady 1964, Warner Brothers. (Reproduced by courtesy of the Kobal Collection)*

## Gender and status

When Eliza hurls Higgins's slippers at him she confounds both the Cinderella and the Pygmalion stories that lie behind Shaw's play. Although both Higgins and (in Act Five) Pickering are flabbergasted by this unexpected transformation, both Mrs Higgins and Mrs Pearce had long ago spotted problems ahead. Do you recall the premonitions of Eliza's question, 'What's to become of me?', in Acts Two and Three? On page 32 Mrs Pearce asks exactly the same question. Unlike her employer, she has a strong sense of Eliza as an individual with a life and rights of her own who must 'think of the future'. When she realizes that Higgins is going to ignore her advice, she limits herself to trying to make the best of the situation. Mrs Higgins, just like Mrs Pearce, is anxious to know 'on what terms' (p.64) Eliza is living at Wimpole Street and the 'problem' she identifies is 'what is to be done with her afterwards' (p.67). Eliza, she says, has been trained in the 'manners and habits that disqualify a fine lady from earning her own living without giving her a fine lady's income'.

## EXERCISE

What do you think has really worried both these sensible women?

## DISCUSSION

The obvious career opportunity for a young woman with these 'advantages' is prostitution, and this is a shadow that has been hanging over Eliza since Act One. It is why she is so extremely distressed to think that she might have been 'taken down' by a detective for 'speaking to gentlemen' – a euphemism for soliciting – an offence for which 'They'll take away my character and drive me on the streets' (pp.13–14). This is why she is so preoccupied with her 'character' (p.17) and maintains both here and in Act Two that she's a 'good girl'. Long before she met Higgins, she'd been trying to better herself (p.14), but it's very much easier for a poor young woman to 'fall' than to rise when not only can her attempts to earn a living be criminally misconstrued, but the most innocent remarks (such as calling Freddy 'Freddy') can suggest impropriety. Even the eminently respectable Clara assumes the worst when a strange man offers to call her a cab.

---

Did you spot this? I wouldn't be surprised if you didn't, because the issue is addressed very obliquely, as you might expect in an age far less publicly frank than our own. The protagonist of another Shaw play, *Mrs Warren's Profession*, made her living from a bawdy-house, although the innocent spectator might well have imagined it was a boarding house. In *Pygmalion* the references are there for those worldly-wise enough to unveil them. Mrs Pearce and Mrs Higgins, both in their way women of the world, are as sensitive as Eliza to how her 'reputation' might be harmed by living with two bachelors in ambiguous circumstances. Shaw seems never to have consummated his own long and not unhappy marriage, and so had a private interest in suggesting that men and women might live together unsexually.

His more explicit motive for contradicting the marriage ending of both the Cinderella and the Pygmalion stories was that he did not believe that marriage in itself was an answer to the question of how a woman who 'comes alive' might live an independent life. Shaw wrote his play when the campaign for women's suffrage was at its height, but even if the vote had been won it is not clear that someone in Eliza's position would have been enfranchised. The campaign was for equal, not universal voting rights, and not all working-class men had the vote at this time either. However, the cards were not just stacked against women in the political sphere: legally, financially, educationally, socially and traditionally they were disadvantaged in all classes of society. As a self-proclaimed feminist, Shaw wanted to see women equally represented everywhere, not just at the ballot-box, and to have concluded his play with a traditional wedding would not have addressed this issue.

The problems of social mobility, which were even more acute for a woman than a man in the class-ridden society on which the curtain rises in Act One, would also have been evaded by a fairy-tale ending. It was eccentric of Shaw to identify phonetics as the key to social mobility; indeed, he has been accused of being frivolous in suggesting that 'The reformer we need most today is an energetic phonetic enthusiast' (Preface, second paragraph) when plenty of more urgent reforms needed attention. But we have already seen how he liked to provoke his audience (or readers) with outrageous statements. What he is implying is that the whole class hierarchy is preposterous and could be demolished by something as simple and apparently superficial as rendering traditional divisions inaudible in people's speech. More seriously, he wanted to 'prove' that education could be as potent a factor in social change as economic power. But does Eliza's education answer the repeated question: 'What's to become of her?' She asks it again in the midnight scene in Wimpole Street (p.78). The alternatives would seem to be a return to her old life or marriage. But unlike Cinderella, her clothes don't turn back into rags: her old clothes have been burned. And she throws his slippers at 'fairy-godmother' Higgins, whose only suggestion is that she 'might marry, you know'.

## Happy endings?

When the curtain rises on the last act, we expect a resolution or denouement (pronounced day-noo-mong) – a term derived from the French, meaning 'unknotting', often used at the end of a story. But if marriage isn't to provide that sense of unravelled ends being neatly tied up which constitutes an ending in so many romances, what is to replace it? Shaw's proposed 'discussion' still needs some kind of ending. Compare the ends of Act Four and Act Five and you might decide that not much happens in the last act. The play *could* have ended with Eliza and Higgins's big row and a dramatic parting at the end of Act Four. The tone is more civil at the end of Act Five as Eliza stalks off to her father's wedding, but we still do not know what will become of her.

So if we make little headway with the plot in Act Five, how does Shaw use the time? What saves the act from being a potentially tedious stretch of argument and recrimination? Surely Doolittle. Here the craft of the 'wright' is very evident. Shaw surprises us and gives a boost to the comic pace. Doolittle didn't seem like a loose end to be tied up. We might have finished with him. But up he turns and with him the conventional happy-ending wedding after all: only it's not that of the hero and heroine – and it's not entirely happy. 'She's been very low, thinking of the happy days that are no more', says Doolittle of his intended (p.97).

This time, however, there's no real battle with the transformed dustman. The kind of verbal fencing that we traced in Act Two here takes place between Eliza and Higgins, left alone on stage while Mrs Higgins dresses for the wedding (pages 98–105).

## EXERCISE

If you have time, go through the dialogue marking it as you did Act Two, and identifying also those points where Higgins changes tack instead of answering Eliza's charges.

## DISCUSSION

Perhaps the key speech is near the bottom of page 100, when Eliza accuses Higgins of being a 'devil' who can 'twist the heart in a girl' and who has always 'got round' his housekeeper. It strikes me that it's not so much Eliza's heart that's twisted as Higgins's arguments. He's cleverer than any of the other characters, and he uses his cleverness to obscure just how devious his arguments are. Sometimes his tactics are childish. Near the beginning he thinks he's scored a point when he says 'I havent said I wanted you back at all' (p.98) and technically he's right. But Eliza is perfectly justified in assuming that was what he meant by asking: 'Have you had enough?' A consummate egotist, Higgins changes Eliza's every retort to his own advantage: the question was *not* whether Eliza has 'ever heard [him] treat anyone else better'; it's highly unlikely that he can 'do without anybody' as he boasts (pp.99–100); his grand claims to 'care for life, for humanity' simply miss the point – and so the sequence goes on. He uses, perhaps abuses, his eloquence to duck away from every point she makes. Just as in the Higgins/Doolittle episode, however, it's difficult to identify quite what either of them is arguing about. Eliza is less skilled than Higgins, but no less determined. Both are really making a stand in defence of their autonomy – their right to be the kind of person they want to be.

Yet I don't think that Shaw plays fair. He gives Higgins some mighty lines which any actor would play to the hilt: 'I have my own soul: my own spark of divine fire' (pp.99–100). And what does he give Eliza? 'Every girl has a right to be loved' (p.102) – a line out of the most sentimental romantic fiction! Doesn't she deserve better than nice-but-dim Freddy? I suspect Shaw of putting his masculine thumb in the scale here, and indeed it has been suggested that Shaw quite deliberately 'punished' Eliza because the actress who originally played her in London, the celebrated Mrs Patrick Campbell, had married a similar upper-crust dimwit shortly before the play's opening, despite knowing that Shaw himself was desperately in love with her! So much for his intention to 'force the public to reconsider its morals'.

How relevant is such personal or biographical information? Some people think that a work of art must 'speak for itself' and that *any* extraneous information is irrelevant. But a more practical point of view suggests that in the production of any work, *three* pressures must combine. Two we have met before, and met repeatedly: the historical context and the artistic tradition. The third might be subsumed by these, but merits separate attention: that is, the life of the writer. In Unit 1 Charles Harrison asked whether Courbet's imprisonment was relevant to his painting. That kind of biographical detail might well be described as a historical, rather than a merely personal, circumstance, but what about the blindness that Steve Regan needed to explain when discussing Milton's sonnet (Unit 2)? Historical and personal circumstances merge, but their extremes are distinct. Shaw's obsessive need to be in control in all his sexual relationships, which Michael Holroyd describes in TV19, surely belongs to his personal make-up. Yet it undoubtedly had an influence on his work. Now there is no magic formula for concocting a play: we can't say that one part frustrated egotist plus a pinch of classical tradition, a dash of social realism and a sprinkling of feminist politics shaken up together will make this particular play; but all those elements are there in some measure, and their deployment is not entirely within the conscious control of the artist.

You could say, for example, that traditional patriarchal attitudes are at least as likely to account for the way in which Shaw, as a male writer, can't quite bring himself to let a female character defeat his own mouthpiece as is his personal chagrin at being jilted. You could say too that when in 1912 there were so few respectable career options for an impoverished woman with middle-class attitudes – such as Eliza had become – it's no wonder Shaw couldn't imagine a satisfactory ending for her. If we were writing this play today we might think of her setting up in business – a whole chain of flower shops called 'Bloomings' perhaps – and taking an Open University degree. But before World War I revealed how many traditionally male occupations could be carried out by women, such a prospect was almost literally unthinkable. Indeed, perhaps the play captures the moment when marriage could no longer be seen as an unproblematic happy ending, but no alternatives were available.

Shaw, however, was not a man to give up an argument, and so he wrote an epilogue to the play, which you'll find on pages 107–119 of the set book. It's a masterly bit of special pleading and in my opinion utterly preposterous. Read it if you have time and see if you agree. It was certainly designed to be provocative. Of course, marriage *to Higgins* would have been a blighted prospect for all kinds of reasons. (It won't surprise you that it's been suggested Higgins and Pickering are gay.) But why not let Eliza 'teach phonetics' as she declares herself ready to do on page 104? The 'biographical' explanation might be because subconsciously Shaw was frightened of the power that might be unleashed when the energies of a clever working-class woman were 'brought to life'. Monsters have a nasty habit of turning on their creators – think of Frankenstein's 'creature'. The sudden glimpse of how Eliza could have delivered Higgins's 'comeuppance' might have been used to supply a wonderful ending. But take a quick look at page 104 and see what Shaw chose instead. Just as he has throughout the scene, Higgins ducks the issue of Eliza's future and takes the credit for her transformation for himself: 'I said I'd make a woman of you; and I have'. There are many things she might say – or even throw – at this moment, but Shaw the arch-creator, the real Pygmalion who has given his characters life, cuts her off with a typical device for ending a scene: the carriage awaits.

What you have in the Penguin text was not the original ending, however. In the original version, Eliza is about to leave with Henry's mother for her father's belated wedding when Henry, 'incorrigible' as ever, dictates a shopping list. He is absolutely certain that despite her protestations of independence she will come back to his bachelor stronghold with Pickering. But 'Buy them yourself', Eliza says 'disdainfully' – and she 'sweeps out'. His mother says she will buy the tie and gloves, and Henry's last line is:

HIGGINS [*sunnily*]: Oh, don't bother. She'll buy 'em all right enough. Goodbye.

It's hardly what you would call a great exit line, guaranteed to bring down the curtain on a roar of applause. The stage direction doesn't help either:

*They kiss. Mrs Higgins runs out. Higgins, left alone, rattles his cash in his pockets; chuckles, and disports himself in a highly self-satisfied manner.*

It's a tall order for the actor. Not only is the curtain kiss exchanged by the hero and his mama, but most actors, left alone to rattle their change, might have more of an air of being left in the lurch. No wonder then that both the stage and film versions of *My Fair Lady* (try saying this with a cockney accent to hear the pun on 'Mayfair') preferred something more like the ending in Pascal's film, which we've included in TV19. There, you'll remember, the director had his Eliza (Wendy Hiller) return silently to a Higgins (Leslie Howard) who has turned his back, but can still (smugly) detect her presence and demands his slippers with every confidence that this time they won't be thrown at him. Shaw's biographer, Michael Holroyd, tells us that Shaw didn't want a 'Romeo' like Howard in the title-role; his decidedly anti-romantic preference was for Charles Laughton. But he accepted Pascal's cinematic judgement, and when he was shown the new ending, only a couple of days before the premier, confined himself to grumbling that 'it is too inconclusive to be worth making a fuss about'.

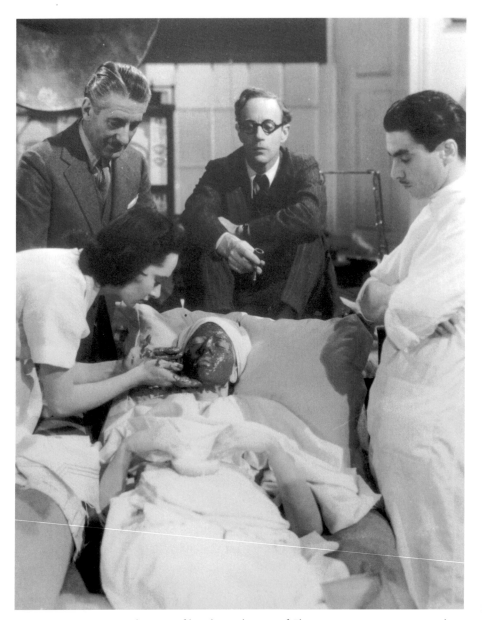

FIGURE 19.7   *In Pascal's 1938 film, the makeover of Eliza receives more attention than Shaw's original text provides. Here she undergoes a mud-pack, observed by Pickering, Higgins and a man in a white coat. What does this suggest about Eliza's relationship with the main male characters? Henry Higgins (Leslie Howard) and Eliza (Wendy Hiller) in the film* Pygmalion *1938, produced by Gabriel Pascal, directed by Anthony Asquith. (The Raymond Mander and Joe Mitechenson Theatre Collection, Beckenham)*

The ending in the Penguin text concedes a wedding – but to chinless Freddy – which happens in the epilogue. The couple's flower-shop needs constant financial support from Pickering's bottomless coffers. Clara, meanwhile, discovers Fabian socialism.

Even this rigmarole fails to provide the conclusion the play could not reach, and in the end I think we have to be glad of this. After all, the characters are fictitious. They come to an end when the curtain falls. We may even want to conclude that a degree of *inconclusiveness* was an inevitable outcome of Shaw's discussion, since there could not, in the historical circumstances of the play's composition, be a totally satisfactory answer to the question of what is to become of Eliza.

I have deliberately brought this week's work to an end in an area of speculation and uncertainty because I wanted to suggest that even the most popular and acceptable works may have unsettling aspects. Indeed, unless a work of art raises a few awkward questions it isn't very likely to be interesting. Next week's work is much more disturbing, and the mild questions about female power that we have touched on here will be eclipsed in *Medea* as we move from comedy to tragedy. Although so much of the material will be new and of a different order, I hope you will be able to take with you and build upon the work you have done here on the nature of drama.

# GLOSSARY

**climax** in a story-line, the high point before a major change.

**convention** traditional practice. The generalized sense of social behaviour which people have agreed to follow (as in 'speeches are a convention at weddings') is paralleled in artistic practices (as in 'plays are conventionally divided into acts').

**denouement** (French, literally 'unknotting') the unravelling of a mystery or the resolution of tensions in the narrative.

**development** in a story-line, the introduction of complications to the opening situation.

**dialogue** speech allocated to the various parts (or characters) in a play for exchange between themselves. When one character addresses the audience or voices thought aloud, this is called a monologue

**exposition** the setting out (or exposure) at the beginning of a narrative of the initial facts needed to make sense of the story-line about to unfold.

**imitation** life-like representation of something by means of another medium (for example, actors representing action and emotions; musical instruments representing raindrops; paint applied to represent light falling on an apple).

**interpretation** a particular 'reading' or understanding of a text or score. This notion of interpretation relies on the supposition that there is no single 'right' way of representing what is significant in a text or artefact.

**performance** the interpretation and presentation of a dramatic text on stage by actors, or the playing of a musical score. Like many of the terms associated with drama, this is a term with a range of meanings.

**realism** theory of the real or representation of what the artist and audience broadly agree is true to life. This is one of the trickiest concepts in the analysis of works of art, and should be deployed sparingly and with caution! Always remember that a work of art offers the representation of reality, not 'reality' itself.

**theme** originally a recurrent melody; by extension, a recurrent topic that is developed during the course of a literary work.

**tradition** time-honoured practice followed, adapted or reacted to by successive writers and artists.

**turning-point** crucial moment or episode in a story-line, which upsets previous expectations.

# REFERENCE

HOLROYD, M. (ed.) (1986) *Major Critical Essays*, Harmondsworth, Penguin.

# UNITS 20 AND 21
# *MEDEA*

*Written for the course team by Lorna Hardwick and Chris Emlyn-Jones*

## Contents

## STUDY COMPONENTS

| Weeks of study | Texts | TV | AC | Set books |
|---|---|---|---|---|
| 2 | *Resource Book 3*<br>*Illustration Book* | TV20<br>TV21 | AC8–9<br>AC10, Bands 1 and 2 | *Medea* |

# Aims and objectives

We have one overriding aim – that is, to help you to read and discuss a Greek play with a sense of discovery and enjoyment. In the course of achieving this, you will be able to:

1   practise and extend your skills, especially in close reading, listening, arguing and reasoning – you will also have the opportunity to take a close look at representations of *Medea* in ancient and modern art;

2   build on the study of drama which you began in Unit 19;

3   consider some of the processes involved in translating a play from ancient to modern in terms of language and cultural situation;

4   develop your ability to make critical use of modern scholarship;

5   discuss interpretation and meaning in *Medea* with awareness of both ancient and modern perspectives;

6   in conjunction with the other material in this block, develop your ability to discuss broad concepts like 'myth' and 'convention' with reference to detailed analysis of particular texts.

# Study note: using the translation

You will see that the line numbers in Philip Vellacott's translation of *Medea* appear at the top of each page. His line numbering is derived from his work on the Greek text, although the line equivalents between the original Greek and the translation are not always exact. Do not worry about this; what is important for your purposes is to be able to locate in the translation those passages which are discussed in the units. The line numbers referred to here have been calculated by counting down from the top from the first line number that appears at the head of the page. Stage directions are a modern addition and are not counted. All lines with an initial capital are counted, regardless of length. (Do not count upwards from the bottom. This sometimes gives a false result!) When quoting from the translation in your assignments, it is good practice to give the line references, and you should use the system outlined above.

When referring you to lengthy passages we have usually additionally given the opening and closing phrases. For shorter passages we have often used the abbreviation 'ff.', meaning 'and the lines following'; for example, lines 17ff. means line 17 and those following. Unless otherwise noted, all page references are to the Vellacott translation in Penguin Classics.

Special thanks to Ruth Hazel and Jenny Marris, Associate Lecturers in the Arts Faculty in the West Midlands Region, who commented on a preliminary draft of this material, and to Simon Spence, Department of Classics, University of Nottingham, who advised on representations of Jason in Greek vase painting. Part of Part 3, Section 3 is based on a pre-performance talk by Lorna Hardwick given at a performance of *Medea* by the Actors of Dionysus in November 1996 and subsequently published in *Dionysus* 6 as '*Medea* – a mystery of family values'.

# INTRODUCTION

For the next two weeks you will be studying the text and performance of a play by Euripides, *Medea*. This was first performed in Athens in 431 BCE, some 500 or more years before the very different public 'performances' or 'spectacles' which you studied in the context of Roman culture in Block 2.

Euripides (pronounced 'Yoo-rip-i-dees') was the latest of the three best known fifth-century BCE authors of tragic drama. The others are Aeschylus and Sophocles. In each case a significant number of their plays have survived, although many have been lost. You will find a brief outline of Euripides' life and information about his other works in Appendix 2.

Although the first part of these units will concentrate on your first reading of the written text in Vellacott's translation from the Greek, remember that the play was created to be performed, so in working on *Medea* you will be building on your study of drama in Unit 19. The complete play is on ACs 8 and 9, and you will need to read *and* listen to it in its entirety so that you experience the play at least twice and preferably three times during the next two weeks. We shall also be referring you to particular passages for detailed study.

The fortnight's work is divided into three parts. The first part will probably take you about eight hours and will concentrate on a first reading of the play. We have built into the workload 'thinking time' for you to reflect on the play and its language. The main aim of this part of the units is to help you with close reading of an ancient text which you as a modern reader may well be experiencing for the first time. A vital part of your work is to listen to the performance of the play on the audio-cassette.

TV20 will explore some of the issues involved in preparing a modern performance. You will see the director, Fiona Shaw, working with drama students to develop their emotional and physical understanding of the relationship between Medea and Jason. You will find it useful to video-record the TV programmes so that you can work with them several times. Before viewing TV20 make sure you are thoroughly familiar with the outline of the plot, and if possible reread the following passages in your *Medea* text:

1 Medea's debate with herself about her sons, pp.49–50, 'Oh, what am I to do? ... The spring of all life's horror, masters my resolve.'

2 Medea's exchange with Jason, pp.30–32, Jason: 'I have often noticed ...' Medea: 'You must know you are guilty of perjury to me.'

The second part of the units will also take you about eight hours. Its purpose is to broaden your understanding of the play by relating some of the main themes to the social and artistic context in which it was first performed. In this part of your work there is more for you to read in the block itself, but you will not be able to benefit from it unless you have carefully read and listened to the play as directed in Part 1. In Part 2 you will also find frequent references back to passages and topics discussed in Part 1. The third and last part of these units will also require about eight hours' study, and will introduce you to some of the judgements made by scholars and critics about Euripides' play. TV21 will help you to compare ancient and modern performance conventions.

In addition to the performance of the play on ACs 8 and 9, which you should listen to as directed as part of your work for Part 1, there is an interactive audio-cassette tutorial (AC10, Side 1, Bands 1 and 2) in Part 3. There is also a television programme to be viewed in each week of study. You will need to refer to *Resource Book 3* throughout these units and to the *Illustration Book* in Parts 1 and 3.

When using the audio-cassettes and viewing the TV, make sure that you study the relevant sections of the *Audio-visual Notes*.

# PART 1   READING *MEDEA* NOW

## 1   GETTING TO GRIPS WITH THE PLAY

The play is relatively short, about forty-five pages in the Penguin edition. There are several possible approaches to reading a new work for the first time. Some people like just to plunge in and read straight through fairly quickly, without pausing to take notes but concentrating instead on gaining a sense of the shape of the play and the development of the action. If you use this method you should ideally also aim to achieve a 'feel' for the language and its effect on you as reader. (What worked for you when studying *Pygmalion* may help you decide your strategy here.)

Other people prefer to progress more slowly, reading and rereading and pausing to make notes as they go. By this stage in the course you may have tried out both methods and be aware of the advantages and disadvantages of each. As you will be expected to read the play twice, you will have the opportunity to use each method but you will still have to decide which to use first! As this is a complete and self-contained text and is not very long, it is well suited to the 'read straight though' approach, so do not hesitate to use that method if you wish. Pay particular attention to the way in which Euripides shows the characters debating with each other. Notice the kind of language used by each of them and *about* each of them. Think about the effect of the pauses in the development of the action, for example when the Chorus reflects on what is happening.

The suggestions that follow are intended to help you with the more leisurely first read. If you follow the swift-read strategy, then you will need to come back to this discussion for your second reading so that you can reflect in more detail on what you have read. I am not going to spend time filling in 'background' information at this stage, but if you simply cannot wait to know more about Euripides or the Medea legend, then look at Appendices 1 and 2 (pp.116–18). However, at this point all you really need to keep in mind is that you, from your vantage point in the twentieth/twenty-first century, will be experiencing a play which was created in the fifth century BCE and which has as its subject-matter events drawn from myth – an imagined story or legend which was well known and part of the received cultural background of the original author, actors and audience.

### Taking notes

By this stage in the course you may feel confident about note-taking, but you might like to refresh your memory from *The Arts Good Study Guide*, ch.2, sect.5, 'Making notes'. Here I will just emphasize three points which are of particular importance in taking notes while reading this Greek play.

## 1 Organizing your approach

The way in which you organize your notes will determine how you 'see' the play, and in turn will influence the way you write about it in TMAs. So make sure that your notes give you scope for a variety of discussions and debates when you return to the play later. When you first approach an unfamiliar text, it is understandable that your notes may be concerned with the 'story' as it unfolds. Of course, you need to grasp the shape of events, but the biggest single difficulty students encounter in writing about literature and drama is that they must *avoid* simply 'telling the story' and instead must be able to comment on the interaction of the characters, on moments of emotion or dramatic decision, and especially on the language and imagery of the text. So make sure that in your notes you emphasize *how* the play is developing, commenting not only on what the action is but on how the issues are presented, how decisions are made, and how dilemmas are communicated. Look out especially for the kinds of language associated with individual characters, whether the words are their own or used by others to describe them. Notice where there are changes in tone and language. This means that in order to produce really useful notes you have to read the text closely and carefully. It would be worth reminding yourself from Unit 2 and the notes you made at that point in the course about the techniques used in close reading. See also AGSG, ch.2, sect.3, 'Reading strategically'.

## 2 Analysing the language of a translation

One crucial difference from the poetry you studied earlier in the course is that you are reading *Medea* through the medium of a translation and not in the original language. This doesn't mean that you will be unable to comment on the language used in the play, but it does mean that, for example, the rhythm and the precise word order you experience are those of the translation into English, not those of Euripides. Don't worry unduly about this now – we shall be thinking about the role of the translation in more detail in Part 3. So when reading and listening to *Medea* look out for the patterns of imagery used – for example, the way in which Medea's feelings and behaviour are sometimes described by others in words usually associated with wild animals. Note, too, which words or descriptions are used to praise and which to blame, which words or phrases convey emotions, and consider how the dramatist uses words to help the audience imagine things beyond its own experience.

## 3 Listening to the play on cassette

*Medea* is a play which is verbally quite demanding, so I suggest that initially you use the audio-cassette in conjunction with your reading of the text. You will find that listening to the performance of the play on cassette will help you to develop your sensitivity to the language, emotions and debates in the play. Listen for the rhythms and emphases in the performers' speech and variations in vocal tone. Think about whether different speakers use different kinds of vocabulary, how they describe and respond to one another, and the effect of the various voices on you. Later in this section I shall suggest a point at which it would be useful to play the cassette while following the text of the play and pausing to add to your notes when you wish. However, you may well find it helpful to listen to the relevant lines on the cassette as you read the opening section of the play, which I ask you to consider in the rest of this section.

### EXERCISE

I suggest you now start by reading lines 1–41 (remember that you should count down from the line numbers given at the top of each page). In all your reading, take note of:

1   who is speaking, and to whom;

2   what is being communicated;

3   *how it* is communicated; this means that as well as taking in *what* is being said, you are thinking about *how* it is being expressed – the words used, the emotions implied, the attitude of the speakers. Of course, as we are reading through translation, it is important to be aware that what we are commenting on is Vellacott's rendering of Euripides' language. Later in the units we will be considering the implications of this.

4   the effect of what is said on others in the play;

5   the effect on you as audience/reader. At this point, what are your feelings about Medea and her situation?

Please read lines 1–41 now.

### DISCUSSION

1   The play opens with the Nurse's speech. She appears to be alone on stage so the speech really has the function of setting the scene for the audience and providing essential background information. (Compare the discussion of *exposition* in *Pygmalion*, Unit 19, Section 2.)

2   She fills in the part of the story which has occurred before the play begins, concentrating on Jason's journey with the Argonauts and his meeting with Medea (see the first note on p.200 of the Penguin text). It was Medea who helped him achieve the tasks he had been set. Subsequently, they both came to Corinth with their children. Now,

however, Jason intends to leave Medea and marry the king's daughter.

3   The Nurse is speaking from a standpoint of sympathy with Medea ('my Mistress'). She emphasizes Jason's treachery and Medea's fidelity and suffering. Strong words are used: 'collapsed in agony' (line 23), 'Scorned and shamed' (line 19). She thus introduces a main theme of the play, the role of women and attitudes to them (lines 13–14). Although Medea is seen as a victim, the Nurse also stands back from the situation and likens Medea to a 'rock or wave of the sea' (line 27) because she will not listen when her friends reason with her. As you read and listen to later scenes in the play, take careful note of the language used by other characters to describe Medea.

The passage also emphasizes the theme of exile. Medea has left her homeland and is alone, even though at Corinth she has 'earned/The citizens' welcome' (lines 11–12). Did you notice, too, that there is an element of fear and foreboding, signalled by the translator's use of words like 'hate', 'dreadful purpose', 'frightening woman', 'enemy'? Note also the idea of 'victory over enemies'.

4   As the Nurse is alone at this point, you will have to wait until the next sequence before assessing her interaction with the children's tutor, the children and with Medea herself.

5   I can't anticipate your reaction! However, make a note of the feelings you now have about Medea and her situation, and try to consider whether they are influenced more by the Nurse's words or by your own attitudes and experience.

## EXERCISE

Now go on and read lines 43–262 closely. On the basis of the notes you make, pause and consider your response to these questions:

1   What is the effect of the contribution of the Chorus of Corinthian women?

2   In what ways do Medea's speeches add to the picture communicated by the Nurse?

## DISCUSSION

1   The Chorus adds another perspective because it is loyal to the House of Corinth (line 138, the reference to the house as essentially Jason's is an interpretation inserted by the translator). However, the women are not fiercely engaged on Jason's side, as the Nurse is on Medea's. They are friendly towards Medea but have a reflective approach to her situation. Notice that this 'distance' also enables them to reflect on the wider moral and religious aspects of the situation. This makes the

Chorus both part of the world represented in the play and part of the commentary on the play (see Unit 19, pp.27–8). They sometimes address the gods directly (lines 148ff.). However, they also act as a foil to enable Medea to express her own ideas and feelings.

(On the cassette the Chorus is represented by one person, a woman. This was the director's considered response to the problem for the modern listener of hearing a Chorus of Corinthian women played by twelve or fifteen male actors frequently singing or speaking together! You can refer to the section on formal elements in Greek tragedy (p.60) for more details about the Chorus in ancient productions, and when you listen to the cassette performance think carefully about the effect on you of the solo female voice of the Chorus.)

2   Medea's speeches express the direct, unmediated force of her emotions. Her language becomes progressively stronger, giving substance to the fears hinted at by the Nurse. However, Medea's reaction is by no means purely emotional. Her speech at lines 214ff. includes a carefully reasoned analysis of the problems faced by an outsider in a Greek city, especially if the outsider is female.

---

It would be useful to read Medea's speech to the women of Corinth through carefully for a second time, and make sure you can summarize the reasons given by Medea in support of her claim that revenge on Jason would be justified. If you are able to participate in a tutorial or self-help group, this would be a good passage to discuss.

Does your own reaction to Medea now still follow the same pattern you noted down earlier? If your view has changed, note down the ways in which it has changed (with reasons if you can).

Please now continue your reading of the play to line 772 (top of p.41). You should pay particular attention to the following passages:

■   The exchange between Creon and Medea (lines 273–356). Consider especially the *effect* of the one-line exchanges in lines 324–343. This technique is called **stichomythia** and is one of the formal conventions in Greek drama.

■   The Chorus at lines 408ff. ('Streams of the sacred rivers ... A new queen rules in your house.')

■   The pair of speeches by Medea at lines 465ff. and Jason at lines 519ff. Note especially the contrast between the social values to which Medea appeals and those used by Jason when he describes what he hopes to achieve by his new marriage. Consider, too, the possible reactions of audiences to these two major opposing statements.

■   Medea's exchange with Aegeus (lines 708ff.) Note the importance of the supplication. Embracing the knees (line 710) is the standard conventional gesture of supplication used in Greek art and literature.

Also important is the way in which Medea's knowledge of medicine/ magic is highlighted. This picks up references to her cleverness and skill in many arts – for example, by Creon, who senses that this is ominous (line 285).

## EXERCISE

At this point, please look back over your notes on your work so far. If you have not already done so, listen to the cassette up to this point. Then draw out the main features of the play's treatment of:

1   expectations about the role and capability of women;

2   the range of language used by different characters to describe a woman's emotions and actions. Notice especially the language used in describing and presenting those who are perceived as 'transgressive'.

It is essential that you do this exercise before reading on, as these issues are the focus of the next section.  ■

# 2  MEDEA'S REVENGE

You have now reached the point in the play at which many audiences and critics experience a shift of sympathy which leads them to take a more critical view of Medea, irrespective of whether they also have a more thoughtful attitude to Jason's position. Vellacott addresses this issue in his introduction (pp.8–9), although he makes a rather facile distinction between 'civilization' and 'barbarism' and does not attempt to consider the relationship between these categories and issues of gender. This section of Vellacott's introduction ought really to be subjected to critical analysis. At this early stage, however, I do not want to divert your attention from the text of the play. So we take up this point later in Part 2.

Please read lines 773–820: from now on, Medea's stance changes. She progresses from perceiving herself as a victim to planning her actions as a pro-active revenge-taker. Her actions are the realization of her own musings and of the foreboding expressed earlier by the Nurse and Creon. Her skills in medicine are to become the tools of a poisoner (line 786). Killing the children is presented as the surest way to injure Jason. (Think about why this might be the case.)

### EXERCISE

Now go on and read and listen to the rest of the play. It would be a pity to interrupt your reading or listening from this point, especially if this is your first encounter with the play. Medea's speech at lines 773ff. has imprinted a sense of inevitability upon events, but the dramatist exploits the episodes which follow in order to build up the tension and to draw out both the raw emotions and the devastating logic which underlie the interactions between the characters. When you have finished the play, make short notes in response to the following questions:

How are events which occur off-stage communicated to the characters and the audience? What effect does this have on their response?

### DISCUSSION

The main communicator of off-stage happenings is the Messenger (especially lines 1135ff.). The intensity of the language and graphic description of the suffering are arguably more affecting than a visual enactment on the stage would have been. The Chorus also has an important role here, both in highlighting the emotional and moral issues (lines 829ff.) and in imagining the events which are taking place off-stage (lines 976ff.).

---

Note that in Greek tragedy the convention was that violence does not actually take place on stage (see Unit 19, p.11). This means that the reporting or description of violence (usually by a messenger) extends the 'space' occupied by the action beyond the physical theatre which can be seen by the audience to an off-stage space, imagined by the writer, actors and audience. To a Greek audience this 'narrated' or 'reported' space was none the less a 'real' part of the action. The technical term for this is *diegetic* **space**.

One emotional and moral issue that the play does not explore is the way that the daughter of the king is herself positioned by male manipulation in relation to Medea and the children. The underlying assumption is that it was 'normal' for women to be disposed of in this way. Female characters in Greek tragedy became interesting to the dramatists when, like Medea, they rebelled against such social conventions.

### EXERCISE

The ending or 'closure' of a Greek tragedy invariably raises particular issues of meaning, so you should now look again at the end of the play (lines 1294ff.). How does the dramatist construct the ending? Which issues are highlighted? Do you find Medea's escape plausible? Do you find it a satisfying outcome to the play?

## *DISCUSSION*

Literally, she escapes in a chariot left to her by her grandfather Helios, the god of the sun. She takes the bodies of the children and is determined that it will be she who performs the necessary religious rites. Afterwards she will take refuge in Athens. Think back to the Chorus' praise of Athens in the patriotic ode (or song) at lines 824ff.

---

The emphasis on religious obligation has a dual function. First, it shows that Medea acts on the basis of religious norms but that she takes over what would, in Greek values, be seen as a paternal obligation. Second, the issue of Jason's moral status is re-argued. Pushing aside Jason's claim that she acted from sexual jealousy, Medea emphasizes that he has broken divinely sanctioned promises: 'Oath-breaker, guest deceiver, liar'. Jason's final lament seems to vindicate Medea's earlier claim that killing the children is the only way to wound him. It also completes the gender role-reversal, since in the Greek system of social values the formal lament was a part of the woman's role at funerals. So the closing sequence demonstrates Medea's escape, both literal and figurative.

The question of whether Medea's escape is convincing is a crucial one. Theatrically, it obviously presents logistical problems for the director and players. There is also the problem of the audience's response. Did you feel that she, in a sense, got away with a crime?

At this stage in your fortnight's work you should now have read the play at least once and listened to the full performance on the audio-cassette. I advise you to put in a second read/listen before starting Part 2. If for any reason you have not yet completed a careful reading of the play and listened to the cassette, this should be your immediate priority.

# 3 FORM AND CONTEXT

Now that you are becoming more familiar with the action and language of the play, I want to ask you to stand back from it a little and address two issues. First, this is the time to draw together various points we noted in discussing how the speakers communicate their ideas and feelings and how they relate to one another – in other words, we can consider the formal structure of the play. Second, you should now be in a position to reflect on ways in which the play seems to be able to communicate directly to us, although we are an audience from a vastly different time and culture, and also on ways in which it may seem strange and remote.

# Formal elements in Greek tragedy

You have already been working with some of the formal elements in your analysis of key passages! To refresh your memory, some examples are listed below in more detail. You should learn the technical names as these will be used in the discussions in Parts 2 and 3.

## Chorus

1   A group of male singers and dancers who performed in the **orchestra** (pronounced 'or-kee-stra'), a circular space in front of the stage (see Figure 20/21.1 on p.71). In mid-fifth-century tragedy there were fifteen in the Chorus, an increase from the earlier number of twelve. Some lines may have been sung by the Chorus leader alone.

The selection and training of the Chorus was the responsibility of the **choregos**, a wealthy man who financed this as a public service. The technical term for what was, in effect, a redistribution of wealth is **liturgy**. This could be used to enhance his reputation, perhaps in the run-up to elections for public office. Recent research has suggested that participation in the Chorus might represent an entry to public life for upper-class young men. The training was strict and they ate together at public expense.

2   The name Chorus is also given to the lyric or poetic sections of the play performed by the Chorus, for example at lines 414ff. The technical term for the choral ode or song is a **stasimon**. However, the first or entry ode has a special name, the **parodos**. The choral odes and dances are usually made up of two matching sections, called the **strophe** and **antistrophe**. *Strophe* is derived from the Greek word meaning turning, and indicates that this was sung as the Chorus turned dancing from right to left. The *antistrophe* accompanied the return of the Chorus from left to right.

## Episode

**Episodes** are the sequences in the play between the Choruses. The dramatic action develops in the episodes, and it is here, too, that the characters develop their feelings and engage with one another and with the issues that confront them. For example, see the section after the entry of Aegeus (lines 661ff). Within episodes, there are a number of formal elements. The most important are dialogue and *stichomythia*.

## Dialogue

A **dialogue** is the formally structured exchange between two characters. It may take the form of a dramatic confrontation, the **agon** (pronounced to rhyme with moan), which consists of opposing speeches such as those between Jason and Medea at lines 447ff. Look back to the reference to 'dialogue as a fight' in Unit 19, Section 3. You could think of the *agon* as a fighting dialogue or contest. In TV20 the director develops exercises based on this approach in order to help drama students get to grips with some of the issues in the play.

## Stichomythia

A form of dialogue in which the actors speak one or two lines in turn. Repetition and echo of words are used for irony or rebuttal. *Stichomythia* (pronounced 'stick-o-mith-ia') can be used to suggest conflict, excitement or to accelerate the pace of the action: for example, Creon and Medea, lines 324ff.

Note also that the actors were professional, unlike the Chorus. All performers were male. They wore masks which covered the face (see Plate 164 in the *Illustration Book*). Originally in tragedy there was only one actor, later two, and finally usually three, doubling to perform all the speaking roles. This came about partly because of the prominence given to the leading role, the protagonist, who was on stage most of the time. *Medea* probably had three actors, although it might just about have been performed by two. There were also non-speaking roles, children, etc.

The fifth-century cultural and political context for the Greek theatre and the conventions of production will be discussed in Part 2. At this point, just be aware that the plays were staged competitively as part of a great civic and religious festival in Athens and that the audience was very large (*c.*14,000 or perhaps more) and included visitors from other states. It is not certain whether women attended.

## Performance issues

The formal elements in the structure of the text present a particular challenge to those performing translations or close versions of the play (see TV20). Some adapters find these disciplines rewarding. Others prefer to put them aside and concentrate on different aspects of Euripides' play, such as the situations and relationships or the shaping of the myth to the cultural expectations of the dramatist's own society. Where this is the case, you will need to consider the effect of such changes because, as you discovered from your first reading, the formal structures and conventions of the play shape the interactions of the characters, the development of the emotional and intellectual force of the play and, of course, its impact on the audience.

In your preliminary reading of the play you experienced the way in which the action is shaped by formal structures. Sometimes this was evident from the way the lines were set out on the page, such as in the choral odes or the one-line exchanges in *stichomythia*. However, the impact of the formal structures of a play is also communicated to us through performance. Important though the text is, the words which have been transmitted across centuries and are now expressed by the translator are only one aspect of the performance. Remember, too, that music and dance were important elements in the performance of a Greek play, although unfortunately we have no surviving musical score or choreography for *Medea*.

### EXERCISE

Which do you think are the most important aspects of performance which do *not* involve speech? Which of these aspects do you think might be particularly important in performing *Medea*? Think especially about different ways in which a centuries-old Greek play might be staged in a modern performance and how non-spoken elements contribute to this.

### EXERCISE

Please look now at the examples of reviews of a modern theatre performance which are included in *Resource Book 3*, D1. These refer to a performance of *Medea* in English at the Lyric, Hammersmith in 1986.

Make a list of the features of the performance which are emphasized by the critics. How many of these would you describe as engaging with the words and mood of the dramatic text?

### DISCUSSION

My list included costume, the stance, gesture and expression of the actors, their spoken tone and vocal effects, the sound effects of the production (including music and screams), stage effects such as lighting and chariot machinery, setting and design, props, type and extent of stage space, presentation of the Chorus, the way in which the translation used (Vellacott's in this production) suggests 'Greekness' or 'modernity' or an uneasy mixture of both, and finally the suitability of the translation for performance. Some of these aspects are closely related to the text, while others are more obviously governed by the conditions of production and the insights of performers and director. All have a part in 'translating' an ancient text into a modern performance.

Most of these features interact with a theme which underlies all the reviews. This is the issue of the assumptions, expectations and prejudices which the audience might bring to the play and the analogies which the performance makes, or which the audience draws, with other aspects of modern society and experience. What is 'alien' to some in the audience may not, of course, be so to others. Did you notice the underlying expectations and attitudes to classical culture held by the reviewers or attributed by them to their readers? Look particularly in this respect at the pieces from *Today* and *The Guardian*.

*Optional reading*: for a wider discussion of a range of modern approaches to the play and the viewpoints they emphasize, read the review essay, 'Monsters and stars: *Medea* in a modern context', in *Resource Book 3*, D2.

# Relationship between Greek and modern contexts of understanding

## *EXERCISE*

Consider the following summary of the play. In your judgement, is it adequate? If not, what would you like to see changed or added?

> The situation which activates the play seems devastatingly familiar to a modern audience. A young woman runs off with a handsome visitor to her country and travels the world with him. They have two children (sons). Her man tires of her and wants a new woman. For his career purposes this has to entail marriage. So his previous partner is rejected, stranded in a strange country having lost out in this relationship as well as having abandoned her old family ties. All this raises her consciousness of the (unfair) differences between male and female attitudes to and experience of marriage. Her resentment of the new bride is mingled with a desire for revenge on the man who has deserted her. She kills not only the bride but also the children. Then she escapes to a refuge, where a new relationship awaits her.

## *DISCUSSION*

I expect reactions to this summary will vary widely. It is superficially attractive because its main features correspond to the outline of the myth, but it leaves out some important aspects. Nevertheless, some of you might have said that this version seems like a parody, although it does 'translate' features of the story into modern idiom. However, transplanting the situations and relationships of a Greek play into a modern context can never be exact, and this description seems to summarize the action at the expense of the particular dynamics of Euripides' play. When compared with the ancient story, this 'version' leaves out the fact that Medea is not merely an outsider at the city of Corinth but is perceived as a barbarian (i.e. a non-Greek). In addition, she was a sorceress, whose skill had enabled Jason to prosper but had also involved the betrayal of her own father.

The rather crude summary above also does not leave room for the mortal/immortal element. Medea is not quite a goddess but is related to the gods. All these elements are aspects of the story which are not easily transplanted into modern cultures, although the outline of the myth and the events of the story can provide a framework for creative adaptation which crosses the cultural gap between Greek myth and the late modern age.

---

Different ages have explored various ways of defining and crossing this cultural gap. For example, some writers and artists in the later part of the nineteenth century made close associations between sorcery, witchcraft and the powerful aspects of the personalities of transgressive women. There are some striking examples in the *Illustration Book* (Plates 172–4 and Colour Plate 70). This kind of construction of Medea also figured prominently in Amy Levy's dramatic poem 'Medea' (1884), in which a new character, Nikias, was added to Euripides' cast list. Nikias' role was to emphasize Medea's 'dark' and 'foreign' physiognomy, her 'wildness' and lack of 'maternal' feeling, in contrast to what he saw as the 'gold hair', 'lithe limbs' and 'gracious smiles' of Glauce, Jason's new wife. Levy, who had achieved the distinction of being the first Jewish woman to matriculate at Newnham College, Cambridge, used this racist stereotyping to create an image of Medea as a demonized victim. You may have the opportunity to consult Levy's poem as part of your information technology work at summer school. The issue of Medea's magical powers is quite difficult for modern performances to convey. In TV20 you can see a workshop exercise which Fiona Shaw developed with drama students to address this very problem.

A modern audience might or might not be inclined to sympathize with Medea because she can be presented as the victim of both gender and ethnic discrimination, a response satirized by *The Times*, which added a byline to a serious discussion of a 1996 performance of the play: 'Crazed illegal immigrant Mum slays kids in cheating hubby's secret love nest'. This is surely not what *Medea* is 'about'. I suggest that there are two crucial questions which jar audiences, both ancient and modern, and perhaps leave them profoundly disturbed by the play:

1   *Why, unless deranged, does she kill the children?* To respond to this question involves judgements about whether she is mad *and* about why she kills them (Euripides probably added this dimension to the myth).

2   *How can she then survive, let alone prosper?* This question requires us to make judgements about how (logistically) she gets away with it and about how she can bear to live on in the knowledge of what she has done.

Euripides, like modern creative writers and adapters, presented an ancient story and its problems through the prism of contemporary language. His handling of the two questions above, which I have identified as problematic, can best be approached by looking in detail at the way he grounds the debates and emotions of the play in the context of Greek values. This involves mapping the interaction between the themes of gender, ethnicity, and civic and religious values. It also requires the audience to enter into a cultural framework which accepts doing harm to enemies, including the exaction of revenge, as morally desirable. This problem of the 'distance' between ancient and modern cultural assumptions will already be familiar to you from your study of the Colosseum in Unit 5. Testing the limits of such frameworks of cultural understanding is one aspect of this play's power in both ancient and modern contexts, and it is these elements which will be the focus of your study in Part 2. In Part 3 I shall return to these problematic questions, so keep them in mind as you work through the next part.

# *PART 2* *MEDEA* AND ITS CONTEXTS

## 1 ENGAGING WITH THE DRAMA

### Introduction

By this stage you should have read the whole of *Medea* and listened to the cassette performance at least once. You will find it useful to give the play another read-through, either before or during this section; in any case you are, I hope, now familiar with the broad outlines and some of the details of the play. Study of Part 2 should take you about eight hours. The approach to the play here will be different from Part 1; instead of reading the play through, we will be picking out details from different parts in order to look at it from one particular angle: how the play might have been received by an audience contemporary with Euripides. The sections which follow consider a number of different ways in which our appreciation of the drama may be increased by an awareness of the physical, social and cultural context of the original performance. Many ages have contextualized *Medea*, and what follows is not a claim that the original context is 'authentic' in the sense of being the only way the play should be performed. The value of investigating the original cultural context, however, is that our interpretation of the play can thereby be placed in a historical perspective which helps to mediate between our experience and that of Euripides' audience. The concept of 'authentic performance' will be introduced later in the course (Block 6, Unit 29), and TV21 (to be viewed in connection with these units) directly discusses the issue both in general and in relation to *Medea*.

### Contextualizing the play

Let's begin with our experience, and in particular our own emotional involvement in the situations, actions and suffering of the characters in the play. Consider, for example, a traditional vehicle for pathos in Greek tragedy, the 'Messenger Speech' (pp.51–5), the account of the horrible off-stage deaths of Jason's bride and her father Creon. In this speech narrative, description and reported speech are combined to generate maximum empathy with the victims – what Aristotle (384–322 BCE), a philosopher and commentator on Greek tragedy writing about 100 years after the first production of *Medea*, described as the emotions of 'pity and fear', which he considered the appropriate feelings generated by the best tragedies. In reacting to *Medea* on this level, we are surely compelled, consciously or unconsciously, to relate our emotional feelings about the suffering of a young girl and her father to our own personal values and those of the society in which we live. Empathy – or even its opposite, antipathy – requires a personal reference point derived from a modern situation or imagined 'scenario'. Such a modern 'scenario' was, you remember, outlined at the end of Part 1, and I would like to use this as a basis for further study.

## EXERCISE

Looking back for a moment at the 'summary' of *Medea* on p.63 and any notes you may have made, consider the modern social issues on which this scenario touches. Briefly, from your memory of the play, try to think of lines or passages in the play which raise these issues in your mind.

## DISCUSSION

Here are three issues raised by the scenario, which may or may not correspond with your personal list, but which do relate to questions prominent in current social discussion and argument. Please briefly note the references – if you have time, read them through.

(a) *Gender relations*. A prominent context here would be Medea's first speech to the Chorus of Corinthian women on pp.24–5; note especially her strongly polarized presentation of male and female social roles as fighting in battle and bearing children respectively (bottom of p.24–top of p.25). This speech is said to have been read at suffragette meetings in the early twentieth century. Look also at Jason's generalized 'male' observations on women and sex (p.34, lines 568–75) and the female Chorus' challenge to the traditional domination of male perspectives in Greek myth (pp.29–30) – a parallel to the idea of 'history written by men for men'?

(b) *Attitudes to children*. Medea's infanticide (p.56); note also the attitude of the Chorus, which perhaps at this point corresponds surprisingly closely to current attitudes to child abuse and parental infanticide. Remember one of the crucial questions for a modern audience, posed on p.64: 'Why, unless deranged, does she kill the children?'

(c) *Ethnicity and social identity*. Medea as 'outsider' and 'barbarian' (p.34 bottom, 'Asiatic wife'); the need for strangers to conform socially (p.24, line 221); Medea as 'exile' (p.35, line 603). See especially Jason's expression of the 'dominant culture' (p.33, lines 533ff.). This seems relevant to modern assumptions about the supposed moral superiority of Western society.

You were no doubt aware of some or all of these issues (and others), explored at length in *Medea,* which interact with your own attitudes and preconceptions, and without this kind of interaction the play cannot come alive. *Medea* owes its exceptional popularity as a play for staging in the twentieth century at least partly to the particular perceived 'relevance' of its central themes. Yet, if we try to take things a stage further – to put our reactions into some kind of context – we will need to explore the nature of the interaction between our attitudes and the totality of what is in, and presupposed by, the play. In particular, we may need to concentrate on elements which, on the face of it, *don't* correspond to what we may conceive as the 'issues'.

Keeping the same headings, let's look for a moment at elements in *Medea* which don't fit the picture sketched out above.

(a) *Gender relations.* Is Medea's presentation of herself in a dramatic context as an 'oppressed housewife' in a male-dominated society (pp.24–5) consistent with her frequently expressed need to punish her enemies, to prevent them having the 'last laugh' (p.41, line 793)? What do you make of the close proximity in the play of the Chorus' revision of male-dominated legend (pp.29–30) and Medea's plan for revenge (pp.28–9)?

(b) *Attitudes to children.* Medea's speech, when contemplating the killing of her children (pp.48–9), presents not only the emotional agony of a mother but also an imperative, which ultimately prevails, that she must kill her sons to spite Jason: 'I understand/The horror of what I am going to do; but anger,/The spring of all life's horror, masters my resolve' (p.50, lines 1074–6). Do you find the coincidence of these two emotional states in the same person, the second of which dismisses the first as the 'soft talk' of a 'coward' (p.49, lines 1049–50), psychologically convincing?

(c) *Ethnicity and social identity.* Medea is presented – in fact, presents herself – as a barbarian 'outsider' who might easily provoke dislike, but is she not also an 'insider' in the sense that she is a 'queen' (p.21, line 118) on terms of easy intimacy with the 'international aristocracy'? She and Aegeus need no formal introduction to each other (pp.37ff.). She has acquired an established place in Corinth, her exiled status earning her welcome (p.17). Yet, when the play opens she has been displaced by Jason's new bride and has no family to fall back on. On the other hand, at the close of the play her isolation and disadvantage have resolved themselves into a spectacular divine escape in the chariot of the Sun god, her grandfather, with the bodies of her children. Her status is signalled visually by her exceptional elevated position above the stage building – a position normally reserved at this point in the play for divine appearances (pp.58–61). The place was actually called the **theologeion** = the place above the stage where the *theoi* (gods) appear. Medea may be an outsider, but of what kind?

Later in this part (Sections 3 and 4) we shall be exploring possible answers to these and other questions.

## Play and myth

Having related *Medea* forwards to our own reference points, let's briefly contextualize *backwards* from the play to the mythical story from which it came. In *Medea* Euripides was creating his own version of part of a traditional story well known to his audience. Variation of incident and detail in the Greek myth, of which the Medea–Jason story is a part (see Appendix 1 for details), is clearly indicated by different versions by other Athenian playwrights and from other Greek poets. Unfortunately, we know very little about these other versions because they survive only in fragmentary form (see Appendix 3), but we know enough to be aware that Euripides took his own line on certain incidents. The most significant of Euripides' variations concerns the infanticide: in *Medea* it is deliberate rather than (in another version) unintentional, and the deed is done by Medea herself rather than (in yet another version) by the family of Creon in revenge for the murder of the king and his daughter (see a hint of this latter version on p.57, envisaged as a dangerous possibility by the sadly deluded Jason at lines 1302–4). This suggests that the playwright wished to put emphasis on his particular treatment of this incident. The evidence of his other plays generally suggests that Euripides was notorious for challenging the expectations, values and assumptions of his own society. The experience of his original audience, therefore, might not have been unlike ours in the sense of involving the necessity of relating and, if necessary, adjusting their everyday values, as well as their knowledge of the myth, to the challenge of Euripides' new presentation. You might like to compare and contrast *Medea* with *Pygmalion* in this context. Shaw takes a myth rather more remote, one assumes, from the knowledge of most of his audience, but, like Euripides, uses it to unsettle their social values and expectations. Is it also perhaps significant that the transformation of the central character in both plays, although very different in each, leads to a problematic conclusion?

# 2  THEATRICAL SPACE

We start with the most basic of all contexts, the physical space in which the play was designed to be performed. Just as the structure and character relationships of *Pygmalion* are inseparable from modern staging which involved the proscenium arch and curtain, so the shape of the Greek theatre profoundly affects how the formal structure of *Medea* was played and perceived.

## The design of the theatre

The theatre at Athens had a distinct design, replicated throughout the Greek world (see Figure 20/21.1, p.71), the parts of which corresponded to distinct elements in the text of the play. What follows recaps and expands on what you learned in the section on formal elements in Greek tragedy in Part 1.

1   The audience would usually have been a large one; as you learned on p.61 many of the population (possibly excluding women) attended (*c*.14,000 at Athens). They sat on tiered seating in the concave semi-circle built into the side of a hill (see the photograph of the theatre at Epidauros in Figure 20/21.2). This is known as the **theatron** (viewing place, theatre). Although from the fourth century BCE this was made of stone (as in the photograph), we have literary evidence that the fifth-century seats may have been wooden.

2   The Chorus occupied the prominent central space (*orchestra* = dancing floor). Much of the Chorus' contribution was sung and danced; about both of these we know, alas, next to nothing. We just have the words, from which it is possible to work out the metrical rhythm.

3   The actors performed on the narrow stage in front of the **skene** (pronounced with two syllables, 'skay-nay', meaning tent or stage building, from which we derive the word 'scene'). The *skene* served as an actor's changing room and a place for costumes and props. The front of the *skene* was used as a backdrop for the play, usually, as in *Medea,* the façade and entrance of a house. In Euripides' time the *skene* was made of wood, and was, like the seating, probably moveable and not much, if at all, elevated above the level of the *orchestra*. This enabled the actors to perform with the Chorus in the *orchestra* as well as on the stage. The elevated stone stages and façades to be seen in many surviving classical theatres are later Greek or Roman; at the back of the stone stage of the Athenian Theatre of Dionysus (see Figures 20/21.3 and 20/21.4), however, can be seen post-holes which held the wooden beams of the original stage.

*You should read the next paragraph in conjunction with Figure 20/21.1.*

Entrances and exits for players in the drama were either from the sides between *theatron* and stage (an area called a **parodos** ) or through a central door in the *skene*. In *Medea* the *skene* represents the façade of Medea's house, and other entrances lead to and from the rest of the town. So Medea and her household use the door of the *skene*, whereas the Chorus of the play, who are present throughout from the moment of their entrance (p.21), enter via the *parodoi* (plural of *parodos*) since, as Corinthian women, they are from the town.

Greek dramas are therefore played out in public or 'outdoors'; what is behind the stage represents a private, domestic area into which the audience cannot see. We shall shortly see that physical arrangements in this theatrical space have important dramatic significance.

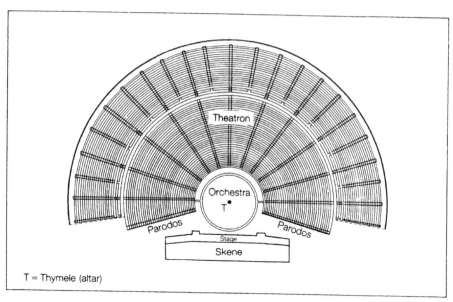

*FIGURE 20/21.1   Schematic plan of a Greek theatre based on the theatre at Epidauros*

*FIGURE 20/21.2   The theatre at Epidauros, dating from the late fourth century BCE; the upper part of the seating was not built until c.170–160 BCE. (Photograph: Ancient Art and Architecture Collection)*

*FIGURE 20/21.3 The Theatre of Dionysus, Athens. The date at which the theatre was first built in Athens is uncertain. There was possibly a major building development in the later fifth century BCE with significant remodelling in the third quarter of the fourth century BCE . There were also many further reconstructions in Roman times and later. (Photograph: Ancient Art and Architecture Collection)*

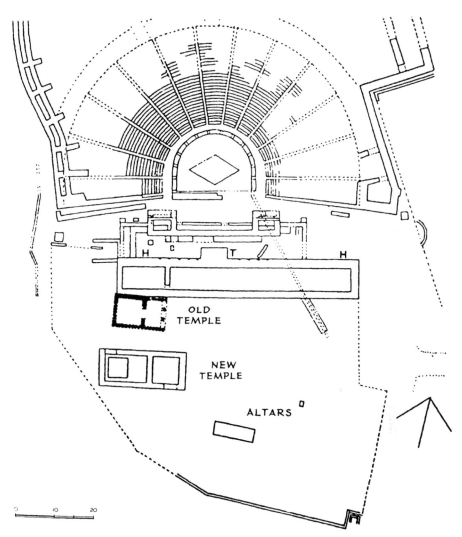

FIGURE 20/21.4    *On this plan of the Theatre of Dionysus at Athens the letter H indicates Wall H, which is a long line of conglomerate blocks with a rectangular platform and slots for beams. This is thought to have formed the base for the stage building, but there is debate about whether it was laid down in the fifth or fourth centuries* BCE. *If it was fifth century, then it may provide evidence about the physical conditions in which Medea was performed. The stage at that time was probably a low platform up to twenty metres long connected by low steps with the orchestra, which was the theatrical space occupied by the Chorus. Reproduced from R.Green and E. Handley,* Images of Greek Theatre, *1995, London, British Museum Press, fig. 13.*

# Medea's first entrance

The first 200 lines of the play are chiefly given to minor characters: the Nurse enters at the beginning of the play through the central door (one assumes from p.19, lines 55–6, though in many modern productions she is often just 'found' on stage). The Tutor must be bringing the children in from the side (he is not up to date with Medea's latest emotional state, p.18, lines 42–5), and the Chorus enters on p.21. However, the scene is interspersed with off-stage ejaculations from Medea; the printed word inadequately conveys the violence of her emotions (Greek: *io, aiai*, normally rendered as shouts and screams), her 'sobbing and wailing' (Chorus, p.23). The menace of her unpredictability is continually emphasized. Yet her first speech on stage is a long, close analysis of the various aspects of what she sees as her position, notable for argument rather than unfettered expression of violent emotion (pp.24–5).

## EXERCISE

Consider for a moment what is happening to Medea from when we last hear her (p.22, line 168) up to her entrance on p.24 (line 214). Has she changed? If so, in what way? Is she 'controlling herself'? Concealing her feelings? How would you explain the change, if there is one? Think about what has been said above concerning theatrical space.

## DISCUSSION

1   It is important not to put too much weight on the stage direction at the bottom of p.23. The texts of Greek plays come down to us entirely without any stage directions; this direction represents simply an inference by the modern translator describing what he interprets as a change in Medea's manner and emotional state based on the obvious difference in tone between off-stage and on-stage speech. 'Medea comes out' obviously describes what happens, but the second sentence is based on an assumption of what has happened off-stage: Medea wiping her eyes and 'pulling herself together'? And don't forget that the person playing Medea would, like all the other characters in the play, have been wearing a mask. Inference from facial expression to emotional state is not a possibility in the Greek theatre.

2   Related to 1, we might, as some scholars have, see the speech on p.24 as an example of Medea's notorious ability, demonstrated on several occasions during the play, to dissemble her feelings and present a calm exterior masking her rage and violent anger (the successful, though difficult, containment of emotion is how the speech seems to me to be played in the audio-cassette). On this interpretation, then, her speech is an effort of concealment – not of her feelings towards Jason (there is no need for that – the Chorus is

friendly and already disapproves of him) but of the depth of her rage. Or is it an example of her versatility, her 'cleverness' (see p.26, lines 291ff.) at being able to articulate her feelings in different ways?

3  The third alternative I would like to discuss focuses not on what Medea is but *where* she is – her physical movement from inside her house into the 'outdoors' of the theatre. This move from private to public is signalled in the text by the use of two very different types of dramatic speech for which Greek uses different types of metre: more lyrical for emotional utterance and a regular dialogue metre for reasoned analysis on stage. It could be argued that the two modes of speech relate, therefore, not primarily to two different psychological states but to two different modes of communicating situations and emotions. These two modes are, in this instance, associated respectively with the private 'indoors' and the public 'outside' – that is, in the social arena.

---

These three interpretations are not to be considered as mutually exclusive: you don't have to choose one and eliminate others. However, 3 is emphasized here because, first, it clearly relates to something we know about the play – how, in general terms, it was staged (whereas psychological states we have to arrive at by inference). Second, Medea's movement between the private and public worlds, indicated by the area 'behind the stage' and the theatre itself, mirrors a basic dichotomy in Athenian society of the fifth century BCE: the polarized social areas of space perceived to be inhabited by women and men. Women were largely confined to the private house, while men engaged in social and political activities which took them to public spaces and buildings.

## The place of the Chorus

On p.56 the Chorus agonizes as Medea kills her children off-stage and suggests (lines 1275ff.) that it ought to intervene. Why doesn't it?

**EXERCISE**

Think about this for a few moments and jot down your ideas.

**DISCUSSION**

Physical fear, you might initially say. Corinthian *women* are not likely to oppose physically someone of the calibre of Medea. Yet the question has wider implications. One of the unbreakable 'rules' of Greek tragedy appears to be that the Chorus never intervenes physically in the action, never goes on the stage or leaves the *orchestra* except to exit at the end.

So that, in a sense, is an answer to the question; the Chorus 'obeys' the rule. But, I think you will agree, this doesn't get us very far. 'Why the rule?' you may ask.

---

The Chorus is one of the most difficult aspects of the play for a modern audience to understand and appreciate. What to do with the Chorus is a notorious 'headache' for modern producers of Greek tragedy; you will have noted that the audio-cassette uses a single voice. If we think of ourselves as readers of the play, we tend to regard the Choruses as subsidiary, almost digressionary. The Chorus comments on the action, gives advice and support, broadens the mythological perspective (discussed in Section 5 below), but remains in the background. Indeed, the Chorus' fictional identity reinforces its inability to intervene: typically it comprises old men, women (as here) or slaves, closely involved in the events but unable to take physical action.

Yet as viewers of the play, if only in imagination, we can see that the Chorus is physically very prominent: literally in the foreground, between most of the audience and the stage, occupying by far the largest part of the acting area (see Figures 20/21.1 and 20/21.2). Unlike the actors, it is also present for almost the total duration of the play, and its exit (given the technical name ***exodos*** – think of our word 'exodus') marks the formal end of the play.

The apparent conflict between physical prominence and marginal relevance to the action suggests that the Chorus has a role quite distinct from that of the other participants in the play, and this point has to be brought out even (especially) when a single voice is used for the Chorus. It is also worth remembering another important distinction: unlike the other actors, who were professionals, the members of the Chorus were chosen from the citizen body of Athens. Thus they appear to have been essentially amateurs (see Part 1, p.60).

A problem with our perception of the Chorus may be the absence of this element in most dramatic traditions with which we are familiar. But we can still try to view the Chorus in terms of modern theatrical conventions, which allow a narrative or commenting voice to interrupt the action – the 'voice-over' in film or TV, the 'narrator' or on-stage commentator on the action (see Unit 19, p.27). Returning finally to our original context – the murder of the children – it is significant that, having failed to step out of role and intervene, the Chorus immediately assumes a typical interpretative position between action and audience, mediating the horrific by universalizing it in the mythical story of Ino, the only other woman, the Chorus says, to kill her children.

# Entrances and exits

As a final exercise in this section, taking the play in conjunction with Figure 20/21.1, try to work out the following:

1   From where do all the characters in the play make their entrance on to the stage? The stage directions don't tell you this, but remember that the *skene* represents Medea's house. The relevant entrances are on pp.17, 18, 23, 25, 30, 37, 51.

2   At what point(s) does Medea exit?

3   What does the use of entrances and exits tell you about the relationship between Medea and Jason?

## DISCUSSION

1   You probably discovered that, with the relatively unimportant exception of the Nurse, all the other characters must enter from the *parodoi*, since they come either from other parts of the town or, in the case of Aegeus (p.37), from another place altogether (not always specified but usually obvious). Medea alone enters from the central door of the *skene,* since it represents *her* house.

2   From the moment when she comes on at line 214 (p.24), Medea does not exit until line 1247 (p.55); she controls the action of the whole play by her continuous presence on stage. She effectively guards the door. When, finally, she does exit, it is to kill her children and in effect to destroy her house. Her only appearance after this destruction is as the transmuted goddess figure of pp.58–60.

3   Jason presumably now lives with his new wife in Creon's palace, and so his entrance (p.30) is not from the central door of the *skene* but from elsewhere. This emphasizes not only his desertion of his family but also his own displacement; *he* may claim that the power and influence have now gone elsewhere (p.30, lines 446ff.), but Euripides' use of theatrical space tells us otherwise. Jason's only attempt to re-enter his former house is his desperate attempt to save – as he supposes – his children (p.57), the futility of which is symbolized theatrically by his vain attack on the door of the palace. But it is too late. Medea, having destroyed her family, leaves her house for a different place altogether, the *theologeion* (p.58).

The purpose of this exercise has been to show how important it is to visualize the use of theatrical space while reading, or listening to, the play. In *Medea* one effect of this use is to emphasize the overriding significance of the house – the private domestic area from which Medea derives her power and from which others, notably Jason, are excluded. In this play what is private is secret and dangerous.

# 3   GENDER

We have seen in the previous section that Medea moves between two social areas: the private area of the house and the public area in front of it. We have also noted that the perception of the private/public divide is closely related to that of another dichotomy: between female and male. Medea's move onto the stage entails, as we have seen, a change to a manner of speech associated with the male world of debate and argument. In an article written in 1968 an American scholar, Kenneth Reckford, tellingly described this as 'Medea's first *exit*' (Reckford, 1968; emphasis added); in entering the theatre, she was also exiting from the private world of her house. In this public area Medea competes on equal terms with her male opponents, and in each case secures her objectives by deploying a range of persuasive techniques. Her success comes from her ability to move at will from argument based on logic to appeals to emotion. For example, she plays on Creon's paternal feelings to extort from him the fatal concession of a day's grace (see pp.25–8). Let's now see how this quality of Medea is displayed in one of the central confrontations of the play.

## Medea and Jason

A significant moment in the play is the elaborate confrontation between Medea and Jason on p.30, extending for almost six pages, in which they state their case against each other. Actually, 'case' is used almost literally here, since the scene is set out as an imitation of an Athenian lawsuit, in which the parties to the 'suit' attempt to assert guilt and innocence by argument and counter-argument. Many of Euripides' plays have this 'set-piece' debate between two central characters (known as an *agon* = contest, from which we derive words like 'antagonist' and 'protagonist'. Remember the description of *agon* as a 'fight' (pp.60–61 above). Note that Jason attempts to answer Medea's accusations point by point; they each have their say and conclude with a shorter, and so more intense, exchange on pp.34–6.

### EXERCISE

Please read these speeches now (pp.30–36). While doing so, try to decide how they each think they are justifying their case. In order to help with this, consider what basic values each is appealing to; what are the key words each uses to attempt to persuade? Look first at Jason, who is the first to speak as 'defendant' in the 'case', then at Medea.

## DISCUSSION

1   Jason's defence has three points: first, to minimize his obligation to Medea in reply to her assertion of his obligation (pp.31–2). Second, he appeals to what he claims is their mutual advantage; in other words, he is appealing to *expediency* ('ensure advantages', p.34, line 566). Third, he also seeks to polarize himself and Medea in psychological terms: *he* is the person who is thinking logically; *she* is all emotion (for example, lines 590ff.).

2   Medea, immediately she speaks (line 465), redefines the argument in terms which explicitly counter those of Jason. Her concern is for honour, loyalty and fidelity to solemn promises: 'You filthy coward' (465); 'My poor right hand, which you so often clasped!' (495). Her speech contrasts with that of Jason in its emotional tone. Manner of speech, in each case, reflects content.

---

Analysis of this section of the play has often been conducted in terms of who can be said to have 'won', or which of the contestants the original audience would have supported, usually with the warning that an audience largely or entirely consisting of Athenian males would not necessarily have given their support on gender lines. For example, a male spectator might have been more influenced by Medea's arguments about the importance of keeping oaths than by the fact that Jason is a fellow male. In practice, deciding on the allegiance of a group of people gathered together on a day in 431 BCE, and whose values are only partly understood, is a tricky business. In any case, the debate is not 'realistic' in the sense that it faithfully reflects anything which could have happened in the real world contemporary with the play; women and men did not (indeed would not have been permitted to) debate in public like this. In this sense the play is removed, in its setting and characters, from real life (see the discussion on social attitudes in Section 4 below).

Yet this very removal from the everyday allows Euripides to bring to the surface tensions in gender relationships which would probably have remained implicit in the society outside the play. In Athenian society the most important male values were concerned with assertive qualities, such as personal honour, bravery in battle, political power and general competitive excellence in a public arena: 'the excellence of a man consists in managing the affairs of the city capably, and so that he will help his friends and harm his enemies' (Meno, a character in the philosophical dialogue *Meno* by the philosopher Plato (*c*.429–347 BCE), articulating a popular view). Women, on the other hand, were expected – in theory at any rate – to live unassertively in private, looking after the household and bringing up their children. *Resource Book 3*, D3 (Lysias) and D4 (Xenophon) are informative on this: please read these short extracts now. However, it is important to note – see the introductions to the pieces – that neither of these is strictly a documentary source; they both have compelling 'hidden agendas'.

Before Jason's desertion of her, Medea showed him traditional obedience; by the time the action of the play begins, however, her attitude has changed. This shift is less clear in Vellacott's translation because his rendering is incorrect; there is a contrast between the past (instead of 'she is all/Obedience', it should say that she *has been* all obedience, lines 12–13) and the present ('But now ...', line 15). It is clear that in certain respects she is asserting values normally associated with men: she sees Jason's conduct towards her as an 'insult' (line 602), and he is a 'lying traitor' (line 618). Her assertiveness and argumentative skill are typical of the men who engaged in political and forensic activity.

What of Jason? His implied rejection of the argument based on honour, which he does not confront directly, suggests deficiency in a key male value. However, what is most obvious in Jason's attitude is his total lack of conventional *heroic* qualities such as exceptional bravery in the accomplishment of mighty deeds, great physical strength, intrepid resourcefulness and endurance in the face of danger. He is a major heroic figure from Greek myth whose status would suggest to Athenians all the positive male virtues writ large – yet he leaves a woman, Medea, to articulate them. He never denies that all his exploits were only made possible by Medea, but her state at the time (she was in the grip of 'helpless passion', line 530) absolves him, he thinks, of the need for gratitude. The absence of the traditional male function in Jason is strikingly illustrated at the end of the play (pp.60–61), where we see that Medea deprives him ultimately of the paternal role by refusing him the bodies of his children for mourning rites (lines 1377–8).

Medea ultimately prevails because she deploys in an extreme way the characteristics of *both* sexes: she is skilled in the male ability to argue and debate, but she also has control of the female private world, symbolized by her control of the door of the house which Jason has deserted. In the next section we shall look at Medea's position more closely.

## Medea: wife and hero

*Medea* has often been called a feminist play; a speech which has made a key contribution to that label is Medea's first appearance (p.24), where she inserts into an expression of her situation a general articulation of the oppressed position of her sex.

### EXERCISE

Please reread that speech (lines 228–50) now, and describe what Medea states as the basis of what she presents as oppression.

## DISCUSSION

The basis of Medea's speech is the exposure of male *power* as something which oppresses women. She also compares the dangers involved in the most fundamental activities of either sex (what more or less defined their existence) – war (along with politics) for men and bearing children for women (lines 248–50) – and stands the conventional valuation on its head: 'I'd rather stand three times in the front line than bear/One child.'

---

We have some reason for supposing that Medea does not, even in this speech, represent an Athenian wife and mother in all particulars (although we need to be cautious about this). The first, rather basic point is that the speech is composed by a male playwright, delivered by a male actor (like the theatre of Shakespeare, women did not take part in the Greek theatre as players), to a largely (or completely) male audience. Within the play itself, also, Medea has her own agenda; she is talking directly to the Chorus, and may be attempting to gain some solidarity with the 'ordinary women' of Corinth while at the same time articulating explicitly male values: 'a man's true character' (line 219); 'a Greek/Should not annoy his fellows' (lines 221–2). There are also jarring social details: an Athenian woman of the time of Euripides did not herself 'buy' her husband (lines 229–30): it was done for her by her father. Nor did a prospective bride herself bind her husband with oaths. But we must remember the mythological dimension: Medea is really a foreign queen with royal, not to say divine, connections.

## EXERCISE

Now please reread Medea's speech on pp.48–50 in which she deliberates on whether she can bring herself to kill her children. There is a tension in the values expressed in this speech; can you say where this tension lies? Compare, for example, lines 1022–38 with lines 1047–51.

## DISCUSSION

Much of this speech reflects the Medea of her first entrance: she envisages all the things she will lose by her children's death: attendance at their weddings, repayment for the pains of childbirth, and someone to perform the burial rites when she dies. Her tender emotional response to their appearance is, however, to be strongly contrasted with her other attitude, expressed later in the speech: 'Are my enemies/To laugh at me? Am I to let them off scot free?' (lines 1047–8). This is the heroic, masculine Medea, embodying traditional Athenian male values of doing good to one's friends and harm to one's enemies. As she says earlier in the play: 'Let no one think of me/As humble or weak or passive; let them understand/I am of a different kind: dangerous to my enemies,/Loyal to my friends. To such a life glory belongs' (lines 805–8). Here, and elsewhere when she expresses such sentiments (for example, lines 394ff.), she is in the tradition of the male heroic model presented in terms of social and military power and success.

---

In the course of the play not only is Jason seen to be deficient in the male gender role, but, as we have seen, Medea herself takes over many of the values and attitudes traditionally associated with it without, however, entirely relinquishing the 'mother' role also.

## EXERCISE

In this speech (pp.48–50) do you think Euripides mediates or explains the tension between Medea the mother and Medea the hero, determined to get even with her enemies?

## DISCUSSION

My reading is that he doesn't really mediate or explain the two personae at all, but simply presents them, rhetorically juxtaposed in the speech, as two warring elements in Medea, the latter of which ultimately wins: 'I understand/The horror of what I am going to do; but anger,/The spring of all life's horror, masters my resolve' (lines 1074–6).

---

# 4  MEDEA THE BARBARIAN

Greece in the classical period (fifth–fourth centuries BCE) consisted of independent 'city states' (the Greek word is **polis**, from which we derive words such as 'political'); Athens was one of these. Greeks generally regarded themselves as more civilized than other peoples, whom they called 'barbarians'. The word actually comes from the Greek *barbaroi*: people who make unintelligible sounds like 'bar-bar', that is, they do not speak Greek. Besides not speaking Greek, 'barbarians' were also considered to lack the advantages of law and civilization, which were felt to be synonymous with the *polis*. Among the Greeks, Athenians considered themselves prominent in this regard. In particular, Athens jealously guarded its citizenship; not long before *Medea* was written, a law had been passed restricting citizenship to the children born from marriages in which the wife was the daughter of a citizen and the husband was a citizen. So Athenian citizens and foreigners could not intermarry unless they were prepared to accept that their sons would be denied citizens' status (see the Athenian law quoted in *Resource Book 3*, D5a, and note the observations in D5b). Possession of citizenship was important since it brought with it many rights and privileges, among them direct participation in the political process, from which other groups, such as slaves and 'resident aliens' (non-citizens living and working in Athens), were excluded.

## Social attitudes

When exploring any evidence for social attitudes in *Medea*, two things must be remembered:

1   Like almost all Greek tragedies, the play is set in the far-off mythical past.

2   The play is set not in Athens but in another neighbouring *polis*, Corinth.

These facts should certainly make us cautious in using the play as *direct evidence* for the actual contemporary social situation at Athens concerning attitudes to foreigners outlined above. However, as we saw above with gender, what we already know from other sources about social attitudes in Athens can be used with caution in exploring the play itself.

### EXERCISE

Please reread the following passages in *Medea* which present being 'foreign':

1   Medea's speech (once again!) on pp.24–5, and read as far as the end of Creon's speech at the top of p.26.

2   The exchange between Medea and Jason on pp.32–4 (lines 495–567) and Jason's comment on lines 1328–30 ('I am sane now ... Into a Greek home').

How is the idea of being a 'stranger' presented?

### DISCUSSION

1   In Medea's first speech her perception of herself as foreign is closely bound up with her exploration of her position as a woman; she is doubly an 'outsider', who is apparently tolerated because her behaviour has conformed to social expectations. But as an exile she is already distancing herself from the Chorus: 'But the same arguments do not apply/To you and me' (lines 251–2), where the differences are the possession of family and friends, which the Chorus has and Medea does not have. The Greeks describe these as *philoi* ('friends' but with a much wider connotation than the English word: those who can be relied upon to help and defend you,

*including* your family). At the beginning of the speech (lines 214–20) there is also a hint, which becomes more explicit in the words of Creon (lines 313ff.), of the association of 'foreign' with 'clever', 'deceitful' and 'dangerous' (see especially first line p.26). Implicit in this is that she lacks the restraints which 'civilization' imposes.

2   The total lack of communication between Medea and Jason in their major exchange lies partly in their differing conceptions of what it means to be a 'stranger'. For Medea it is a question of loss: sacrifice of family and bitter regret (lines 500–7). For Jason, in the notorious passage on lines 533ff., it is a question of being or not being Greek, with all the 'advantages' which that entails. Jason returns to this point (the contrast between Greek and non-Greek) in his anguish at the end of the play (lines 1328–30): 'I was mad before, when I/Brought you from your palace in a land of savages/Into a Greek home'.

---

Note also that at the bottom of p.34, line 591, 'Asiatic wife' translates literally as 'barbarian bed'. Once again, though less explicitly here, the 'ethnic' and 'gender' themes are intertwined.

## Medea as 'stranger' and 'guest'

In line 221 (p.24) the word 'stranger' translates the Greek *xenos*. What the translation does not indicate, however, is that the word indicates not so much a person as a relationship: a *xenos* is not only a 'stranger' but also a 'guest' or 'host'. In other words, it denotes the normal relationship of hospitality between someone needing shelter, food, etc., and someone under an obligation to provide it because asked, an obligation taken very seriously by the Greeks. An example of another translation of *xenos* which illustrates this point neatly is on p.35, where Jason offers Medea letters of introduction to 'friends' (line 613, repeated in contemptuous refusal by Medea at line 616). These would have been people able and willing to take over the obligation of 'hosts' to Medea as '(stranger-) guest'.

### EXERCISE

Consider for a moment how your knowledge of the nature of this relationship between a stranger and a host might be used to develop our interpretation of the quarrel between Medea and Jason.

## DISCUSSION

Euripides continually lays emphasis on Jason's betrayal of Medea as a breaking of 'sworn oaths' (line 439 by the Chorus). This is not just like the breaking of marriage vows in a modern context; it is, in part, the betrayal of the mutual relationship of *xenia* (a noun derived from *xenos* and often translated as 'guest-friendship'). The importance of oaths is clear from the scene with Aegeus (pp.39–40), where Medea can be certain that Aegeus' oath will protect her in Athens, no matter what she has done, and Aegeus can conveniently use his oath as an excuse for not surrendering her. Jason's abuse of hospitality is emphasized by his casual attempt at passing on the *xenia*-obligation (p.35) – he personally, of course, no longer has this problem because of his marriage into the ruler's family. In their final bitter exchange of recriminations, Medea calls him 'guest-deceiver' (line 1393). His action contravenes a basic law of conduct, and breaks a bond between them which, in a sense, gives a logic to Medea's subsequent actions – the need to revenge herself upon those who have now, since no longer *xenoi* (plural of *xenos*) and so 'friends', become 'enemies'.

---

# Medea and Athens

Athens enters the play as the *polis* whose ruler, Aegeus, offers Medea a refuge and so completes her plan of revenge on Jason. Medea binds Aegeus by performing yet another act which was used to establish a bond between two people – supplication (see p.56 above), which involved the supplicant touching the knees of a potential protector. (Medea reveals that Jason had supplicated her in the past when he was desperate – see p.32, lines 495–6 – and note the key role supplication plays in Medea's persuasion of Creon on p.27.)

Not unexpectedly, Athenians tend to be represented in tragedy, if at all, in a favourable light; when Athenians appear, they are invariably the 'goodies', and the unpleasant events which make up the plots of the genre tend to happen elsewhere, as in *Medea*. Here, where the Chorus emphasizes the beauty, favour of the gods and intellectual distinction of the city of Athens (pp.42–3), the contrast is made explicit. No doubt there is a sense here in which the audience would have perceived the Chorus stepping out of their character as Corinthian women and becoming the Athenian citizens which, in real life, they were.

## EXERCISE

Please reread the Chorus which celebrates Athens (pp.42–3). How does the Chorus view Medea's plan, and what does this tell us about the way Euripides presents her relationship with the city?

## DISCUSSION

The key point lies in the transition from the first two sections of the Chorus to the latter two: Medea as a child-killer cannot be welcome in Athens. She will bring a pollution, something which was seen as akin to a real and contagious disease spread by people who murdered family; a polluted person had to be kept out to avoid the anger of the gods falling on the whole community.

---

We have already seen above how the presentation of Medea as 'barbarian' foreigner brings into play implicit contrasts with the 'civilization' of the Greek *polis* and, above all, Athens. It is all the more strange, therefore, that at the end of the play Medea announces she will proceed to Athens, having established religious rites 'to expiate this impious murder' (line 1384). Is a deal with Aegeus (pp.37–40) and a promise of expiatory rites (see previous sentence) sufficient to make polluted, barbarian Medea welcome at Athens? How is the conflict resolved? Does Medea simply get away with the crime – to repeat a question already asked?

When studying *Medea* we need to be continually aware that it is not a documentary source but a play, with conventions which are intended to serve the creative aims of the playwright. Yet this does not exclude the possibility that the playwright may have wished to heighten in his audience awareness of a particular contemporary social issue: what does it mean to be an outsider? His unconventional treatment of an established story exploits its status in popular consciousness to add an extra dimension of uncertainty to what may have been perceived as traditional values.

## EXERCISE

As a final exercise in this section, and to recap the last two sections, please read pp.8–9 of the Introduction to *Medea* by the translator, Philip Vellacott (from the third paragraph, p.8, 'To appreciate ...', to the end of the section). While doing so, ask yourself:

1   How does Vellacott explain what he perceives as the basic distinction in the play – between civilization and barbarism?

2   Do you consider that his explanation adequately characterizes the play, as you have studied it so far?

## DISCUSSION

1   Vellacott sees the opposition in fifth-century BCE socio-political terms: Athenian feelings of cultural superiority, characterized by control and order (Jason) against barbarian excess (Medea). The play explores

the way in which 'civilization', inflexibly conceived, contains the seeds of, or leads to, excess.

2    Here I have two reservations, one general and one more specific:

(a)    I am always suspicious of an analysis of a drama which contains the words, 'The lesson of ...' (p.9, line 15). A play is not a parable; we cannot assume that the play contains some 'moral' easily encapsulated in a sentence or two.

(b)    In any case, is the 'civilization/barbarism' theme exclusively what the play explores? What Sections 3 and 4 have suggested is that the tension between Jason and Medea relates to more specific issues connected with Greek values of guest-friendship (*xenia*) and the importance of promises. If we look back at these, it appears that Vellacott's polarized view doesn't really reflect the play: Jason's predicament arises from his neglect of Greek values which, as a Greek hero, he might be expected to support. And Medea's behaviour appears to be partly motivated *not* by her 'barbaric' qualities but by an inappropriate adherence to conventional Greek male values: helping 'friends' and harming 'enemies'. This last point leads into a further issue with which the 'civilization/barbarism' polarity is inextricably linked: gender (which Vellacott doesn't address). A key aspect of Jason's position is the distinction between the male heroic role he might conventionally be expected to play and the reality: reliance on Medea for his past exploits, displacement from his house (even physically) and denial of fundamental paternal rights (burial of his children). Medea's assumption of these Greek male roles complicates her position as, ostensibly, a barbarian 'outsider'.

---

It might be thought unfair to criticize an introduction confined to two-and-a-half pages for what it leaves out; however, what I would like you to take away from this is an awareness of the inevitable distortion involved in 'monolithic' explanations of a complex dramatic work coupled with a failure to consider it in terms of the values expressed in the text. In Part 3, Section 2, you will have an opportunity to look at a modern scholarly article which explores these issues further.

# 5  MYTH AND PLAY

So far we have been looking at contexts within the play itself and what we can safely deduce about social and moral values, and the immediate physical circumstances of performance in the theatre. In the next two sections we will be casting the net wider to see what light can be cast on

*Medea* by exploring some external factors, starting with the story, or cycle of stories, from which *Medea* came.

Greek tragedy is created in relation to a variety of contexts outside itself, and one of the most important aspects of this 'outside' is the vast store of myth and legend from the Greek past. This past forms the subject-matter of almost all Greek tragedies which have come down to us. The events are placed in a distant past, and the political and social context is, on the surface at least, far removed from that of the audience (fifth-century Athens had no kings, queens or princesses). Playwrights maintained their individuality not by creating totally original stories but by selecting and emphasizing particular aspects or details of a myth, by choosing a particular tradition from a variety of alternatives, and even by inventing particular events, if appropriate. So, for example, as we have seen above (p.69), the idea that it was Medea who killed her children and that she did the deed deliberately is very likely to be Euripides' own invention, and this suggests that he wished to give this event particular emphasis. At the same time, as we have seen with *Medea,* Greek tragedies contain continual reference to contemporary society (see, for example, Medea's first speech on p.24).

*Medea* then, like other Greek tragedies, has a 'dual focus': it inhabits two worlds, that of the mythological past and also the Athenian present. This means that the playwright, in selecting his story and treatment, is inevitably making a personal statement about 'the past' (the mythical material) and his attitude to it (that is, his 'present'). Let's examine in detail what this means for *Medea.*

## The good ship *Argo*

*Medea* is Euripides' version of the last part of an old and important cycle of myth known as the Argonautic legend, the story of Jason and the voyage of the Argonauts (for the full extent of the story, see Appendix 1). We know that the cycle was old from a reference in Homer's *Odyssey* (eighth century BCE), one of the two oldest surviving Greek poems. This briefly mentions that the voyage of the ship *Argo*, captained by Jason through the clashing rocks from the land of Aietes (father of Medea), was 'celebrated by all' (*Odyssey,* Book 12, lines 69–70). The Athenian audience would have been generally familiar with the mythical background; Euripides tends to use the start of the play (the Prologue) to inform the audience which particular part of the myth he is dealing with, in order to indicate his particular starting point and to put them in the picture about events leading up to the beginning of the play.

**EXERCISE**

Please now reread the first speech of the play (pp.17–18). Consider how the events are presented, and think about the significance of the identity of the presenter. For details of the myth, see Appendix 1 and the note on p.200 of your translation.

**DISCUSSION**

The details of the voyage and the events surrounding Medea and Jason were, in many respects, 'neutral' in ethos: they could, for example, be presented as a romantic adventure (princess falls in love with handsome hero and, under the influence of that love, uses her powers to save him), as they were in the later Greek Alexandrian poem *Argonautica* by Apollonius of Rhodes (third century BCE). In Euripides, however, the mythical details of Jason and Medea are not simply recounted but expressed as part of a regrettable series of incidents leading up to the present bad situation (lines 1ff., 'If only they had never gone!'). The myth and love affair are realistically portrayed in the light of the 'morning after'; it is surely not accidental that the presenter is a minor character of low social status, the Nurse, who is in a position to know intimate, realistic details without heroic gloss. The voyage of the Argonauts is regarded not as part of Greece's glorious past but as a calamity.

Jason and Medea are also introduced in specific ways: Jason has betrayed his lover without whom, as we learn later in the play on his own admission, he would have been unable to perform his heroic deeds; Medea has, in her infatuation, murdered her brother and deserted her family. She has blood on her hands already.

Right at the beginning of the play, then, Euripides very clearly establishes a questioning – even negative – attitude to the mythical past.

# The Chorus and the past

One of the roles of the Chorus in this play, as in most tragedies, is to place the events in a broader setting through the sung interludes (*stasima*) between the dialogues (episodes). Here also the play presents an angle on the past.

**EXERCISE**

Please now read two Choruses (pp.29–30 and pp.56–7), and in each case consider two questions:

1    What is the Chorus talking about?

2   What significance does the immediate context have for the Chorus'
    speech in each case?

1   First Chorus: at this comparatively early stage of the play the Chorus
    is expressing its perception of how the events have turned mythical
    stereotypes upside down; instead of a succession of 'bad women',
    men are the deceitful sex. This is presented as a reversal of nature
    ('Streams of the sacred rivers flow uphill'). The Chorus is saying that
    the mythical past has been selectively interpreted by men. In reality,
    infamy has been evenly distributed.

    The context here is significant; there follows the big debate between
    Jason and Medea (see pp.78–80 above), which the Chorus might
    appear to be anticipating (Jason's betrayal, lack of honour, heroism,
    etc.) But look for a moment at what goes before the Chorus. Medea
    makes a speech (lines 364–407) in which she celebrates her deceiving
    of Creon, muses over the most effective way of murdering her
    enemies (Jason included, at this point), and glories in her sex's
    capacity for evil: 'We were born women – useless for honest
    purposes,/But in all kinds of evil skilled practitioners' (lines 406–7).
    Does this not throw an ironic light on the Chorus' sentiments which
    immediately follow? By emphasizing Medea's 'schemes' (line 369),
    isn't the playwright actually undercutting their attempt to even the
    score?

2   Second Chorus: this second example is from near the end of the play.
    The chorus is speaking in great agitation as Medea is killing her
    children off-stage, and it relates this deed to a mythical precedent of a
    child-murderer – Ino, who at least had the excuse of having been
    rendered insane by a god. Is it also perhaps implying Medea's
    insanity here? The Chorus emphasizes the exceptional nature of the
    deed and makes quite clear what its attitude is to Medea now, and
    women in general: 'O bed of women, full of passion and pain,/
    What wickedness, what sorrow you have caused on the earth!' (lines
    1292–3). The Chorus tells us that Ino committed suicide; is Euripides
    here using the mythical tradition to add to the theatricality of the final
    scene by preparing his audience for the *wrong* denouement?

# The sun god's granddaughter

In the final scene of the play (pp.58–61), Euripides executes one of the
bold theatrical strokes for which he was famous. Medea has entirely
abandoned her 'maternal' persona, and has appeared in the place and at
the point of the play normally reserved for a divine 'epiphany'

(manifestation), the *theologeion* (see p.68 above). She is elevated above the sorrowing Jason, though they continue (or conclude) their antagonistic relationship. Medea, godlike, announces what needs to be done and what the future holds for Jason. In her new (or old?) persona she seems to have dissociated herself even from what she herself has done ('this most impious murder', line 1384). The myth has been resumed.

## EXERCISE

Please reread the final scene (pp.58–61), and consider what effect it has on the overall presentation of Medea and Jason.

## DISCUSSION

My conclusion is that in this scene, and especially in Medea's removal to a plane of semi-divine existence, Euripides, far from resolving anything, elevates to a grand scale the contradictions in *Medea* which we have been observing throughout the play. He seems to be reintroducing details of the myth – the burial of the children and expiation – in order to produce a deliberate conflict between the tradition and his version of the story.

In the final scene something seems to have happened to the character of Medea. Here we see only the vengeful sorceress; what has happened to the mother? Jason, on the other hand, shows pitiful anguish at the loss of his children and, as Medea reminds him, the destruction of the woman by whom he might have had more ('You grieve too soon. Old age is coming,' says Medea, line 1397). To what extent do you think that there is a partial reversal of roles? If Medea has ceased to be a mother, is Jason now the one who cares, or at least would like to assume a paternal role in giving his sons rites of burial? Does this reversal affect how we interpret the play?

---

Perhaps it is significant that almost the last lines of the play are given to Jason, and he ends the play in a manner strikingly reminiscent of the opening – a wish that none of it had happened: 'Would God I had not bred them,/Or ever lived to see/Them dead, you their destroyer!' (lines 1413–15). Is Euripides here signalling a wholesale rejection of the world of the myth in favour of an exploration of reality? The short final Chorus does nothing to resolve the situation; the summary seems rather inadequate – perhaps simply a way of getting the Chorus off the stage. Our suspicions may be confirmed by the fact that these words turn up at the end of several other plays by Euripides as some kind of 'all-purpose' closure.

# 6 PERFORMANCE

On the whole, so far, we have concentrated on issues internal to the play itself, or we have used generally established details of the layout of the theatre or Athenian social values in order to clarify structures within it. On occasion, however (see especially pp.78–80), we have found ourselves considering issues like how the social context might have affected reception of Medea's or Jason's arguments, and this inevitably involves us in conjecture, in a general way, about the attitudes of the contemporary audience given, for example, their composition: the likelihood that they were all or mostly men. In the final section of this part, we will be looking at the external context with the admittedly limited brief of considering in what ways it might help us better to understand the play.

## The competition

Performance of Greek tragedy was part of a religious festival to the god Dionysus held in the spring in the presence of a large audience of Athenian citizens and non-Athenians, Greek and non-Greek, who gathered in the Theatre of Dionysus in the centre of Athens (see Figure 20/21.3 – but note that the theatre we see today largely dates from the Roman period). The occasion was competitive in the literal sense: playwrights entered tragedies in groups of three followed by a lighter drama known as a satyr play. The three tragedies could be presented either as parts of a single story or as plays loosely connected by theme; we know that *Medea* was of the latter kind though we know almost nothing about the plays which accompanied it. The entries were placed in order by a panel of judges chosen from the citizen body, the winner being awarded a prize. There is some evidence, again very scanty, that plays were also staged in theatres outside Athens.

It is one of the more tantalizing pieces of information we possess that *Medea* came third and last in its particular competition – tantalizing because we know nothing whatever about the plays which beat it, and have absolutely no evidence as to the criteria the judges applied to their decision of the winner.

### EXERCISE

From your study of *Medea* so far, what do you think might have caused this adverse, or at least less than favourable, judgement?

## DISCUSSION

We might be inclined to conjecture either that: (1) Euripides' dramatic treatment of the theme was considered too radical for average taste – there is no evidence that the judges were other than ordinary citizens; or that (2) his blurring of the boundaries of conventional gender and social roles offended the audience; or that (3) they found his negative or violent perspectives on traditional stories disturbing; or that (4) they did not appreciate his implied ironic slant on Athenian civilization – or, indeed, a combination of any of these four.

# Euripides and 'public opinion'

The word 'conjecture' was used in the previous paragraph because there is very little firm evidence for how the audiences received Euripides' plays. Around 90 or 100 of them were produced in the course of a long career (*Medea* is one of the earliest of the eighteen or nineteen which survive), but he appears to have won first prize only four times (on Euripides' life and works, see Appendix 2). I speculated above that 'negative or violent perspectives' might have been relevant to his lack of success, but *The Bacchae*, produced shortly after the poet's death in 406 BCE and, in different respects, quite as disturbing as *Medea* and considerably more violent, won first prize (possibly respect for the recently deceased?). When he died Euripides was in exile in Macedon to the north of Greece (we don't know why), and Athens was coming to the end of a highly destructive major war in which it was defeated by its *polis* rival Sparta (situated in the Peloponnese, another part of Greece) – a war which had started in the year (431) in which *Medea* had been presented.

Evidence for a view of Euripides is found in two plays of the comic dramatist Aristophanes, *Frogs* and *Women at the Thesmophoria*, in both of which Euripides features as a character. A general point to note is that Aristophanes is writing comedy, with a strong vein of topical satire, and so his portrayal of Euripides should not automatically be taken as a faithful portrait.

## EXERCISE

Please now look at the extracts from Aristophanes in *Resource Book 3*, with their explanatory introductions (D6 and D7). (Note that the line numbers provided relate to the Greek original text rather than the translation. To identify the line references below, count *down* from the nearest line number; it doesn't work if you try to count up.) Then do the following:

1   List the features of Euripides which appear to be highlighted.

2   Consider how, or whether, you could apply them to *Medea*.

## DISCUSSION

1   The extracts from *Frogs* (D6), which was produced shortly after
    Euripides' death – hence the jibe that the playwright has only recently
    reached the Underworld – indicate awareness of aspects of style and
    technique. Aristophanes described Euripides as a 'classy poet'
    (*Frogs*, line 72 – the Greek is *dexios* = intelligent, sophisticated). The
    heart of the comedy is a competition between Aeschylus (525–456
    BCE), an older, more 'weighty' poet, and the 'light' Euripides, in which
    their lines (see the end of extract (iii)) are literally weighed! The first
    line of *Medea* (line 1384) is, on rather bizarre grounds, found to be
    'lighter' than Aeschylus', and so of less worth. Extract (ii) adds a
    further dimension, drawing attention to Euripides' Prologues which
    set the scene and tell the audience what to expect (line 946) – and
    note Aeschylus' 'comeback' here in line 949: 'They knew before they
    came.' Aristophanes notes Euripides' spare use of language, which
    seems to be connected with his argumentative style and – an often
    repeated accusation – the introduction of 'down-to-earth' treatment of
    the characters in the traditional story. Aristophanes also draws
    attention to Euripides' questioning approach (lines 971ff.).

    Euripides is also a character in *Women at the Thesmophoria* (D7),
    here facing a prosecution before a court of women for his portrayal
    of them 'obsessed with sex, drink, lies and gossip/beyond saving, a
    plague to all ... *man*kind' (extract (ii), lines 392–3). This reputation is
    comically seen to be responsible for male caution and repressive
    attitudes to their wives (lines 394–426). It is important to repeat that
    Aristophanes was composing comedy, a genre which, like tragedy,
    has a complex relationship with social reality. However, we can say
    that Aristophanes was at least likely to be drawing on Euripides'
    popular, perhaps joking, reputation among drama audiences (and
    remember that this would have been the vast majority of the citizen
    population).

2   You have read only one Euripides play, and clearly Aristophanes'
    criticisms have all the others in mind as well, including many which
    we no longer have – a large majority. But I think that we can relate
    some of what Aristophanes says to *Medea*. The 'logical argument'
    (*Frogs*, lines 953ff.) suggests the formal *agon* (contest between Medea
    and Jason, pp.30–36), and the down-to-earth treatment of situations is
    related to Euripides' sharp focus on the domestic tensions of the play
    rather than a more distant, heroic perspective on the story (which
    was Aeschylus' popular reputation). Euripides' anti-women reputation
    might have come not only from Medea's character and behaviour in
    general, but more specifically from such lines in the play as: 'We were

born women – useless for honest purposes,/But in all kinds of evil skilled practitioners' (lines 406–7).

---

There is evidence that already in Aristophanes lines like this (unfortunately there are no convenient examples actually from *Medea*) were taken and quoted out of context as *bons mots*: witty, often subversive epigrammatic sayings suitable for use in other literary contexts, with the original context forgotten or ignored; later Greek scholars even made anthologies of choice examples from Euripides.

We are ourselves all too familiar with the popular reputation of prominent individuals built on selective quotation: 'You've never had it so good'; 'There's no such thing as society'. Perhaps, however, the most significant fact about *Medea* is how quickly, after the initial lukewarm reaction, the play as a whole became popular, as evidence from vase paintings illustrates. These works of art (Plates 166–9 and Colour Plate 68 in the *Illustration Book*), which date from the century following *Medea*, suggest not only the popularity of the myth but also specific details from Euripides' treatment, such as Medea's murder of the children and her escape in the dragon chariot. The theme continued to be popular with artists and patrons later in antiquity (see Plates 170–71). So perhaps *Medea* was notorious in the sense of combining official disapproval with a strong and growing attraction for 'advanced' taste.

# *PART 3* WORKING OUT *MEDEA*

The aim of this final part is to help you reflect on the 'modern' and 'ancient' perspectives which you have experienced and to give you some practice in the integration and critical assessment of these perspectives. You are advised to allocate about eight hours to this part. The bulk of the work comes in Section 2. Section 3 helps you to draw the threads together.

## 1 TRANSLATION

The main study-medium of your work for this section is AC10, Side 1, Bands 1 and 2. You will also need your *Medea* set text, the *Audio-visual Notes* and *Resource Book 3*. You should allow about one to one-and-a-half hours for your work on the cassette and the associated activities.

By now you will be well aware of the role of the translation in constructing a bridge between the ancient text and the modern response to the play. The translator is not merely seeking English equivalents for Greek words and phrases. He or she also has to take account of the range of meanings and suggestions which Greek and English words have in their respective cultural contexts (as discussed in TV20). Inevitably, translators have to take decisions about meaning and equivalence. They also have to transplant into a language and culture distant from the original the patterns of allusion, nuances of reference and range of associations which are in the original text. The technical term for the originating text, in this case the Greek text of *Medea*, is the *source* text. The word *source* is also used to indicate the *source* language (Attic Greek – the Greek generally used in Athens at this time) and sometimes the *source* culture (that of Athens in the fifth century BCE). The language into which the translation is made is called the *target* language, which is part of the *target* culture, which includes both the specific occasion and purpose for which the translation is made and also broader issues about the expected horizons of understanding of the anticipated readership or audience and the society of which they are a part. The target language is sometimes said to bend the source language to its need. Perhaps the reverse can be true also. The translator has to negotiate the relationship between the two languages.

Side 1, Band 1 on AC10 identifies various approaches to creating a modern translation of *Medea* and discusses possibly competing demands, such as literal rendering of the original, literary fluency, communication in modern idiom of ideas and emotions, recognizing and bridging the cultural 'gap' between ancient and modern. The participants have all recently produced translations of Greek plays into English, and they debate key questions about the processes of translating texts to be *read* and texts to be *performed*. You should read the biographies of the participants in the notes for AC10 now.

Side 1, Band 2 shifts the focus to you as reader or audience of a translation and considers ways of reading *through* rather than *in* translation. Reading *through* translation involves you in constructing meanings by working with a text in which key words are discussed in the original rather than after being interpreted by the translators. This approach preserves for you the way in which the language used in Greek tragedy is itself a field for debate and struggle.

Both bands of the cassette enable you to compare different versions of important passages in *Medea*. There is also an optional exercise which invites you to have a go at 'translating the translation' for an audience of your choice.

# Extracts from translations of *Medea*

## AC10, SIDE 1, BANDS 1 AND 2

Please turn to AC10. Listen to the discussion on Side 1, Band 1, and in Band 2 pause as directed to refer to *Medea* in Vellacott's translation.

## EXERCISE

As a follow-up exercise, now please read the relevant passage in Vellacott's translation, lines 249–62 ('I'd rather stand three times ... no bloodier spirit').

Then compare the language, tone, speakability and overall effect with the translations produced by three of the participants in the panel discussion:

1  *Resource Book 3*, D8a: James Morwood, *Medea*, Oxford, World's Classics, 1997.

2  *Resource Book 3*, D8b: David Stuttard, *Medea*, Actors of Dionysus, 1996.

3  *Resource Book 3*, D8c: David Wiles, *Medea*, as performed at the Gate Theatre, 1986.

Finally, read the same passage (*Resource Book 3*, D8d) from the work of the nineteenth-century poet and translator Augusta Webster, *The Medea of Euripides: literally translated into English verse*, Macmillan & Co., 1868. This translation won praise at a time when the work of women translators was not generally admired by critics. Webster also wrote a dramatic monologue, *Medea at Athens* (included in *Portraits*, 1870), which explored Medea's feelings when she learnt of Jason's subsequent death. As you read this translation, consider the effect which the somewhat archaic language may have on you as reader/audience. What points strike you in comparison with the other translations you have read? ■

## List of Greek words referred to in AC10 on translation (in order of appearance)

| Transliteration (how the Greek sounds in English; – makes a long vowel sound) | Meaning | Greek |
|---|---|---|
| *gunē* | woman | γυνή |
| *eunē* | bed/sexual relations | εὐνή |
| *lechos* | bed/sexual relations | λέχος |
| *apokteinō* | kill, execute | ἀποκτείνω |
| *phoneuō* | murder, slaughter (verb) | φονεύω |
| *philos* (sing.) *philoi* (pl.) | friend, household, family | φίλος φίλοι |
| *erōs* | love, passion | ἔρως |
| *sōphrosynē* | moderation, level-headedness | σωφροσύνη |
| *echthroi* | enemies | ἔχθροι |
| *kardia* | courage | καρδία |
| *thumos* | heart | θυμός |
| *bouleumata* | plans | βουλεύματα |

# 2 DEBATES IN MODERN SCHOLARSHIP

## Introduction

In this section we shall be continuing the integration of ancient with modern perspectives by exploring another modern approach to Euripides' *Medea*: the scholarly 'article' or 'paper'. Debate between scholars is important in all academic areas. You have already encountered examples earlier in the context of modern history in Block 3. Engaging in this kind of debate is a key skill which it will be essential for you to develop for your future studies.

We are going to read 'A woman's place in Euripides' *Medea*' by Margaret Williamson (*Resource Book 3*, D9). This short article started life in 1985 as a contribution to a classical journal, *JACT Review* (the journal of the Joint

Association of Classical Teachers); as often happens with individual articles, it was subsequently incorporated into a collection of essays concentrating on a particular Euripidean topic (*Euripides, Women and Sexuality*, edited by A. Powell, Routledge, 1990).

The article's paragraphs have been numbered in the *Resource Book* to make it easier for you to identify the many detailed references to it in this section.

## EXERCISE

Please start by reading the first five paragraphs of the article carefully, doing two things:

1   Note any concepts or ideas which you don't fully understand at first reading; it might be helpful to underline these. Some words/ideas that I thought might need explanation are included in the box overleaf, which covers the whole article (don't be put off by the occasional Greek; it is all translated).

2   Consider how far these paragraphs actually cover ground and explore ideas you have already encountered (especially in Part 2, Section 2 above). Don't bother with the footnotes at this stage.

## DISCUSSION

I hope that, in reading this short extract from the beginning of the article, you recognized some of the ideas explored in the section on theatrical space and how this relates to gender and power.

The fifth paragraph throws a particularly interesting light on our earlier discussion of theatrical space in Part 2 (the section on entrances and exits); there I emphasized how, visually, Jason had been displaced from the centre – the house behind the *skene* – leaving power with Medea as guardian of the central door. Williamson's interpretation, however, throws a different emphasis on the spatial dynamics of the play.

## EXERCISE

Please look back at the section on entrances and exits (pp.77–8) and compare with para. 5 of the article; consider what the different emphasis might be.

## DIFFICULT OR UNUSUAL WORDS/CONCEPTS

Structuralist anthropology: analysis of society in terms of relationships which indicate an interlocking structure; anthropological movement associated with Claude Lévi-Strauss (b.1908).

*Oikos* and *polis*: 'household' (including property, family and slaves) and 'city state'; often used together, as here, to indicate 'private' as opposed to 'public' in Athenian society.

Discourse: manner in which thought is verbally expressed; often used in 'structuralist' analysis (see above) in a semi-technical sense to indicate the way in which a particular manner of speaking, choice of vocabulary, etc. represent a distinct social category.

Semantic: an adjective which describes something standing as a symbol or a 'sign' (Greek *sema*) for something else; for example, as in this context, the arrangements of the theatre are seen as 'standing for' or 'signifying' social structures.

Anapaests: a metrical rhythm of Greek verse associated with 'lyric' speech, as opposed to the metre of dialogue.

Registers: the particular types of discourse (see above) selected by a speaker. For example, see paras 16 and 17 for analysis of the different 'registers' selected by Medea in her exchange with Creon.

*Sophia*: Greek = wisdom.

Stichomythic: *stichomythia* is a technical term for the swift exchange of lines between actors in Greek tragedy (also explained in glossary).

*Philoi*: Greek = friends (*philia* = friendship) but with a wider range of reference than the English word; includes extended family, social and political supporters (also explained above, p.83).

Sophoclean hero: a reference to the tragedies of Euripides' older contemporary, Sophocles (496–406 BCE), whose plays tended to feature male characters who exhibited the strong physical and mental qualities thought to be characteristic of a hero.

## *DISCUSSION*

Comparing *Medea* with tragedies by other playwrights, Williamson here explores not the power and influence of Medea's base – the hidden area behind the *skene* – but its anomalous character; it is a 'no-man's land' which derives its 'problematic quality' from Medea's nature and situation as a barbarian.

Note how the tension between the conclusion of this paragraph in the article and the discussion on pp.69–78 above extends and deepens perception of the spatial dynamics of the play. Medea is seen to be powerful, but the play also throws into question the basis of that power. This spatial anomaly forms the basis of Williamson's interpretation of Medea's role in the play, which we will look at shortly.

# The procedure

## EXERCISE

What I would like you to consider first, however, is how the article differs in basic procedure from, say, the discussion of *Medea* in Part 2. I realize that 'procedure' can be a vague term; what I mean here is not the content of the argument or the extent of the ground covered (we shall come to that in a minute), but the point of departure and the manner in which the argument is conducted. Reread, for example, the first two paragraphs of the article and the short fourth paragraph; consider too the significance of the presence of footnotes at the end of the article – you don't need to have read them!

## DISCUSSION

The main points about the article are that the author emphasizes:

1   That it is her personal approach; she is interrogating the source material (*Medea*) in order to produce an original argument. Note that the fourth paragraph gives you the map of the article, as it were (readers of modern articles are not always so lucky!).

2   That this approach is not plucked out of the blue, but stimulated by (see the author's first words) recent applications of structural anthropology and feminism to ancient Greek society and drama (see the two works cited in the second paragraph). She tells us clearly 'where she is coming from'.

In contrast, the study of contexts for *Medea* in Part 2 did not contain this personal aspect or discussion of modern scholarship. This does not mean, of course, that modern approaches were ignored, making the discussion there somehow more 'objective'; it is simply that in an introductory study it is more practical and convenient to follow a more straightforward procedure and leave the apparatus of scholarship implicit.

# The argument

## 1 Structure

Now please read through the remainder of the article, starting with para. 4, and using the author's scheme there to work out which parts of the article relate to her 'three things'.

1   The dividing line between Sections 1 and 2 you may not have found easy to draw, since the author does not signal it in any formal way. In fact, there is no hard and fast line, but para. 11 is summing up and refers back to a quick survey (paras 7–10) of a number of contexts from the play. The following paragraphs (beginning with para. 12) indicate where the main emphasis of the middle section is going to lie: 'the early scenes with Creon and Jason' (beginning of para. 13 – as promised in the fourth paragraph).

2   The middle section is the longest, consisting of detailed analysis of these 'early scenes', leading to a demonstration of the way in which the 'dislocations' in Medea's presentation of herself are closely related to the infanticide (paras 26–7).

3   The final section is signalled in para. 28 where, towards the end of the paragraph, the author directly addresses her third question: what the play seems to be implying about Medea's use of language.

There is also a conclusion (paras 30–34) where the author stands back, as it were, and broadens the scope of the paper to consider other related dichotomies: passion/rationality, female/male.

We have, for convenience, split up a continuous argument, but note in particular how the argument progresses by building one section upon another. For example, see paras 18ff. where the analysis of the 'persuasive rhetoric' of the scene with Creon (paras 13–17) is used to prepare us for the 'registers' of the Jason–Medea *agon.*

## 2 Content

Time does not allow a comprehensive analysis of the whole paper, though your tutor may wish to take up other aspects; here I shall concentrate on a central point. In a paper with a 'structuralist' approach, the characters in *Medea* are analysed in terms of their relationships. In para. 13 *three* types of relationship between Medea and other characters are distinguished. What are they, and what are their characteristics? (This is simply a comprehension exercise on the paragraph.)

## DISCUSSION

1    Blood relationships: these are fixed relationships between people *un*equal in status, such as parents and children; they are characteristic of the private sphere.

2    Exchange between equals: these are fluid relationships, and characteristic of the male, public sphere.

3    Unequal, changing relationships based on a change in status brought about by ritual, which establishes obligations between the participants, such as supplication or guest-friendship (Greek: *xenia*).

## EXERCISE

The author goes on to apply this analysis to the Medea/Creon scene (*Medea*, pp.25–8). Please now reread the Medea/Creon scene with Williamson's commentary, and work out exactly how Medea presents 'the full range of these types of relationship' (para. 14) in what she says to persuade Creon.

## DISCUSSION

The beginning of Medea's appeal (p.26) is presented in abstract and judicial terms: observations about the disadvantages of appearing clever (reminiscent of her first speech on p.24), and an argument about her not having done an injustice to Creon personally and his family (middle of p.26). Here she presents herself as being in relationship 2 above. Creon is not impressed. Williamson (end para. 14) points out that this speech is 'partial in that it takes no account of personal feeling' and contradicts Medea's attitude towards Creon expressed a few moments earlier (line 273, 'enemies'). (Do you think Williamson is correct in assuming that Medea intends Creon to be understood as included among her 'enemies' here?)

Next comes the supplication (line 324). This is relationship 3 above (between the 'two poles' of private and public – and note the reference (para. 15) to how the relationship is physically and visually signalled, here possibly heightened by the toing and froing of *stichomythia*; never forget the impact of the play as a *visual* experience). By this action Medea has now put Creon under an obligation to her.

Finally (closely linked in the play with the supplication) Medea appeals to relationship 1, family ties (lines 343–8). Note that the relationship is not direct (Creon and Medea are not related), but the appeal is 'to Creon's feeling within a parallel relationship' (near the end of para. 15). His feelings for his daughter are manipulated by Medea in order to change his attitude towards her and her children.

## EXERCISE

Having done this analysis, I would now like you to consider two further points:

1   How does Williamson describe the links between Medea's 'registers' (see box on p.100) in this scene? Look particularly at paras 16 and 17.

2   How does Williamson relate this presentation of Medea to the main action of the play? See paras 21 and 23.

## DISCUSSION

1   Williamson makes the point that the links are really not there: 'discontinuities' is how she twice describes them (middle of para. 16 and beginning of para. 17 – see also near the end of para. 17: 'dislocation', 'linguistic gap'). She also emphasizes the 'gulf separating [Medea's rationalistic arguments] from the voice we first heard from within the house.' Is Williamson perhaps implying that Euripides presents Medea as *impersonating* the discourse of different social groups at different times in order to present herself in different ways?

2   Williamson shows how the 'dislocation' between 'registers' implies a lack of stability in Medea's own perception of her role in the play (para. 21). This can be related to her history before the play starts: the betrayal of her own family (para. 23) removes the central relationship to her family (relationship 1 above). Medea is forced to 'take her stand ... in an area where the relations involved are more fluid and ambiguous' (towards the end of para. 23), that is, relationships 2 and 3. 'Medea can only be defending this much less clear-cut and less stable category of *philia*: the central area, and the one with which we would expect her, as a woman to be associated, is absent' (end of para. 24). By this 'central area' Williamson is referring to Medea's blood relations; her father and brother are dead and her children shortly will be also. Indeed, Williamson goes on to relate this dislocation closely to the infanticide in para. 26. Medea has already 'subverted' the distinction between private and public on which her heroic stance rests; in terms of the structure of the society presented in the play, she belongs nowhere. In addition, Williamson makes the particular point that, in a sense, Medea has herself discredited her own language: 'It is inevitable, therefore, that the

consequence of her entry into the house should be wordless violence – the murder of the children who are the most stable measure of its central relationship' (end of para. 27).

---

In concluding this section, note how Williamson's interpretation of Medea, while ranging throughout the play, grows out of the core argument stated at the end of para. 5 (and discussed above on pp.99–100): Medea's social dislocation is seen to be also physical and verbal. Discussion of motivation and 'character', a notoriously slippery concept in Greek drama, is thus grounded in what Medea and others say. By relating this to well-established categories of Athenian social life, the paper avoids one possible accusation of 'subjectivity': the arbitrary importation of our own psychological or moral categories of judgement into what we understand by 'character'. The author uses modern theory as a stimulus, but the essence of the paper is how that theory works out in detailed practice.

## A footnote on footnotes

I have left until last consideration of the 'Notes' at the end of the article. These have a definite function or functions in the construction of the argument.

### EXERCISE

Please look at these now, and consider what main functions they have.

### DISCUSSION

I detect three main functions:

1   Citation of secondary sources relevant to the argument (the most common). These references will include works which the author has read as a stimulus for her own article.

2   More extended discussion in order to supplement or disagree (see n.11).

3   Inclusion of further references to *Medea* (see nn.12, 15 and 16).

---

The important thing to realize about notes is that they should be as they are here, *supplementary*; they support the argument, give information as to further reading, etc., but they are not essential to the argument. Note that two works which are given particular weight are included in the body of the text (para. 2).

## Further reading (optional)

If at this point you have time to spare, you might read an article which approaches *Medea* from a different angle: 'The infanticide in Euripides' *Medea*' by P.E. Easterling (*Resource Book 3*, D10).

# 3  RESPONSES TO THE TWO DISTURBING QUESTIONS ASKED IN PART 1

On p.64 I asked you to keep in mind two crucial questions which underlie possible ancient and modern responses to the play. These questions were:

1   Why, unless deranged, does she kill the children? (The murder of the children is, after all, most probably Euripides' own addition to the myth.)

2   How can she then survive, let alone prosper?

These questions make the play both disturbing and potentially subversive of ordered social and moral values. I want to examine these two questions to tease out the strands of the play through which Medea's state of mind and the reasons for her actions are explored. To suggest she has reasons is not, of course, the same as saying she was justified. The paragraphs which follow represent some of my own thoughts on the subject, and the headings should help you to consolidate earlier material in the units. Apart from a few references to other evidence about Greek social values, the discussion does not introduce any new material. The aim is to draw together material relevant to the two questions set out above, and to give you one response against which you can test the responses which you yourself have developed. There are no 'right' or 'wrong' answers here. *The main aim of this section is to enable you to review your own judgements by comparing them with the suggestions I have included here.* In particular, as you work through the material, think about the differences and similarities in the possible responses of ancient and modern audiences. The subheadings should help you here, but bear in mind the difficulties of *generalizing* about the actual responses of any audience whether ancient or modern. Remember, too, that although *Medea* was written and performed in fifth-century BCE Athens, the setting is Corinth in the heroic age, and the story and characters are from myth. This means that the cultural setting is somewhat indeterminate. The Greek audience had to engage with the relationship between the heroic values associated with their cultural past and the civic or *polis* values of their cultural present. Similarly, a modern audience has to respond across both Greek and modern spheres of reference.

Now please read on, pausing where indicated to refer back to the play and to earlier sections of these units. Above all, pause to think and to note points which you would like to discuss at summer school or with your study centre group.

Euripides adapted the ancient myth in the context of the performance conventions and cultural context of his own time. Nowhere is this more significant than in Medea's first main speech to the Chorus of Corinthian women. In this passage there are a number of key words which are being manipulated for dramatic effect. They draw on a web of associations and layers of meaning in Greek culture and present particular problems for the translator, who has to make decisions which may narrow the range of meanings which can be expressed in English.

## 'Outsiders' in Greek culture

The sections on pp.66–8 and 83–5 above alerted you to plays on the words 'stranger' or 'foreigner' in order to indicate someone who is an outsider. The Greek word is *xenos*, from which we derive 'xenophobia', fear or hatred of foreigners. However, in Greek culture the associations of the word *xenos* were not so limited, nor were they primarily those of inferiority or alienation.

In *The Odyssey* of Homer (eighth or seventh century BCE), for example, *xenia* or hospitality to strangers is an important social value, a quality displayed by Menelaus to Telemachus and by Penelope to the disguised Odysseus. *Xenos* is a word used for host as well as guest, and *xenia* requires observation of the conventions of reciprocal behaviour between hosts and guests. These conventions are flouted by the suitors, who consume all the food in Odysseus' house, rape or seduce the serving women, and vie for Penelope's favours. Justice required that the suitors were punished for these abuses. In Greek culture Homer occupied a place which combined that of the Bible, Shakespeare and Dickens as a source of popular reference and allusion, so Euripides' audiences were thoroughly familiar with the episode and its moral lessons.

Later, and more formally, *xenos* also signified a guest-friend. Guest-friendship was an institution through which the élite from different cities developed a formalized ritual exchange of gifts and obligations. By the sixth and fifth centuries BCE this was sometimes recorded in inscriptions and could play an important part in diplomatic relations.

The cluster of associations surrounding *xenos* and *xenia*, therefore, implies reciprocal relationships between people from different communities. So Medea's acceptance that a *xenos* must conform or adapt (backed up by the Nurse's praise of her at the beginning of the play) carries with it an assumption that she, too, has the right to invoke reciprocal obligations.

Think about the extent to which it is possible to transplant this situation and its implications into a modern sphere of reference. The experiences of the actors in TV20 are relevant to this point.

## Values of the Greek *polis*

Medea further emphasizes her claim by the fact that she addresses her plea to fellow members of the community of the city (not, as has sometimes been translated, to fellow countrymen or fellow Greeks). This immediately places her speech within the value system and rhetoric of the fifth-century *polis* – the society of Euripides and his audiences. She takes up this theme (at lines 252–4) when she contrasts her situation with that of the women of Corinth, who belong both to a city (*polis*) and to their father's home (*domos*). The allusion is not merely to the physical space occupied by the *polis* but to its institutional culture and social organization, which regulated and assured people's lives.

This emphasis on the relationship between being a member of both civic and family communities is a common theme in Greek literature. A very early model appears in Book 9, lines 105ff. of Homer's *Odyssey* when the life style of the Cyclopes is unfavourably contrasted with 'civilization'. According to the poet, the Cyclopes, unlike the Greeks, had no ships, no settled agriculture, no institutions, no meetings for councils and no shared laws:

> Each one is the law for his own wives and children and cares nothing about the others.
>
> *(Homer: Lattimore (trans.), 1965)*

Such a situation is outside the norms of Greek communities. In describing the way in which she is placed outside the protective institutions of the *polis* – she is, in effect, *apolis* (line 254) – Medea indicates *not* that she herself has transgressed expected behaviour, but rather that her conformity has not brought her the expected reciprocal benefits of protection against abuse and injustice. The emphasis on justice (*dike*) is associated with a key point in the early part of the play on oath-breaking and perjury. The notion that Jason's oath to Medea is binding is another indication that his behaviour, too, must fulfil his obligations to her. Her final insult to him is one of 'Oath-breaker, guest-deceiver, liar' (line 1393). In Stuttard's translation (1996) the language emphasizes the seriousness of the rupture of religious sanctions: 'You have broken solemn oaths and sullied all the sacred ties of friendship.' Jason's conduct places him outside the protection of the gods.

## Greek marriage conventions

Medea's claim that she is entitled to demand that Jason stand by his obligation to her is partly prompted by the fact that since she has cut herself off from her father's country, she is not protected by the patriarchal structures surrounding Greek marriage. She therefore has to speak and act on her own behalf. Women's security, both before marriage and after marriage ended, rested with their male relatives. The more elevated the social position, as with Glauce, the more important the marriage as a means of securing alliances, male heirs and the transmission of property. Medea's complaint that 'When, for an extravagant sum, we have bought a husband, we must then accept him as/Possessor of our body' (lines 229–30) transfers to herself the activation of the commercial transaction of the dowry, normally undertaken by a woman's father or closest male relative. In a conventional situation, the corollary was that if the marriage came to an end the dowry was reclaimable, together with the responsibility for the woman. This guaranteed her security. Medea's 'dowry' was her skill and cunning, which are used by Jason to further his career, *and* her reproductive capacity. When the marriage ends, she reclaims what she brought to it.

Thus Medea's speech to the women of Corinth does not deal primarily with her emotional reaction (which is foregrounded elsewhere in the play) but with the civic wrongs done to her. Vellacott's translation, 'touch her right in marriage, and there's no bloodier spirit' (lines 262–3), expresses this more precisely than Warner's (1944) rather anodyne, 'Once she is wronged in the matter of love'. A recent translation by David Stuttard (1996, discussed in AC10) rightly emphasizes the conventionally Greek heroic values on which Medea draws: 'But when she has been slighted in her marriage and her sex, there is no force more murderous.' Avenging dishonour was a traditional heroic male value. It underlay, for example, the Greek expedition to Troy, when they besieged the city for ten years to recover Helen. She was the wife of a Greek leader, Menelaus, and she had eloped with Paris, one of the sons of the king of Troy.

Look back to the discussion on pp.78–80, and think about the similarities and differences in the effects on ancient and modern audiences of the *agon* between Jason and Medea (lines 446 ff.).

## Friends and enemies

It was in the structural and regulated aspects of marriage that the woman could expect to be protected by her blood relations and friends (*philoi* – that is, those with whom her male relatives were in alliance). The giving and taking of a woman in marriage could also be part of an alliance between *philoi*. On leaving her father's house the woman entered another not as a blood relative but as a stranger, albeit a stranger protected by reciprocal obligation. If the marriage was repudiated, this might indicate that the alliance between friends had turned into a feud between enemies, and Greek values insisted that people should do good to their friends and harm to their enemies. By ending their relationship,

Jason becomes, in effect, Medea's enemy. In the absence of her male relatives, her claim on him requires that she herself take responsibility for avenging the insult done to her and this entails harming him. (Refer back to the discussion on pp.80–2 and AC10.)

It is therefore logical, if extreme, that she kills his bride. Furthermore, this value system also explains why she kills his children. This is hard for modern consciousness to understand, although some critics have commented on Euripides' psychological sureness of touch in conveying the propensity of a parent to harm a child in order to hurt the marriage partner. There have been recent modern examples of this in which the father explained killing his children because he felt the state had given all his rights over them to the mother.

Conversely, there may be a temptation to read this as a maternal act to save the children from harm, but in Greek terms this is a misleading reaction. Once Jason has become Medea's enemy, hurting him can legitimately involve harming the heirs of his property and his name. Ironically, a patriarchal value system indirectly sanctioned Medea's action. Greek opinions about the relative biological roles of father and mother are not certain, but there was a view which held that genetically the father's sperm was wholly responsible for the growth of the child, with the mother merely a temporary incubator (Aeschylus, *Eumenides*, lines 658–61).

## Child-killing in Greek myth

There are many examples in Greek myth and folk-tale in which children are killed by men as an act of aggression towards the father or for some other reason. Later in his career (415 BCE) Euripides explored in *Electra* the cultural importance attached to the male line and the resulting implications for the friends/enemies dichotomy. In this play (which is included in your set book) the situation is an equally contentious one. Clytemnestra justifies her killing of Agamemnon as revenge for his sacrifice of her daughter Iphigenia in order to gain a fair wind for Troy. She says that Agamemnon would not have sacrificed his son Orestes in comparable circumstances:

> No: he'd have killed me if I'd touched
> His son; he killed my daughter – why should he not die?
> I killed him. I took the only way open to me –
> Turned for help to his enemies. Well, what could I do?
> None of your father's friends would have helped me murder him.
> *(Euripides: Vellacott (trans.), 1963a, lines 1043–7)*

The Chorus' response to Clytemnestra is crucial:

Your words are just; yet in your 'justice' there remains
Something repellent.
*(lines 1050–51)*

Think about the extent to which modern societies accept that it is allowable and/or desirable to do harm to one's enemies. How might enemies be defined? Are there legal and/or moral limits on the harm we might do to an enemy? Are there *any* modern situations you can think of in which killing the children of one's enemy *as a deliberate act* might be accepted, although still regarded as horrifying?

## Justice, the gods and Medea's escape

Alongside the repellant, there is an awful ironic justice in Medea's action. She tells Jason that her appeal is to Zeus, the guarantor of oaths, who 'Knows well what service I once rendered you, and how/You have repaid me' (lines 1353–4).

In Stuttard's (1996) translation she says, 'but Zeus, the Father, knows not only what I've done to you but what I've done *for* you as well. You were not to humiliate my marriage and my bed while you yourself enjoyed a charmed life, ridiculing me with mocking laughter.'

However, there is no direct divine intervention in the play. Even the closing comment of the Chorus – 'Many matters the gods bring to surprising ends./The things we thought would happen do not happen;/ The unexpected God makes possible' (lines 1416–18) – may be a later addition to the manuscript. Just as Medea has to take on herself the responsibility conventionally exercised by male relatives/friends in order to avenge the wrong done to her, so she herself intends to fulfil the religious requirements due to her sons, and she escapes in the chariot bequeathed to her by her grandfather, the sun god Helios.

The language and imagery associated with the sun are closely interrelated with the action of the play and are symbolic of Medea's identity as a figure who has more than human powers. This brings me to the second of the 'disturbing' questions I asked: once she has killed the children, *how can she then survive, let alone prosper?*

Medea does not escape because she is 'justified' in her actions. Although her actions are explainable, there is no sense of moral triumph, of divine vindication. There is, however, a sense of *heroic* triumph in the Greek sense. The word 'heroic' refers to the values and life style of the warrior leaders of the Homeric poems, *The Iliad* and *The Odyssey*, and the mythical characters of Greek tragedy. Like a hero Medea has, after all, defeated and humiliated the man who insulted her. She has, in a sense, de-heroized Jason. Although it cannot be said that she killed the children in a fit of divinely induced madness, she has gone through an almost literally heart-rending process of decision and action and pays a terrible price in suffering. (See TV20 and 21 and pp.80–2 above and especially

Medea's speech at lines 1021ff.) Yet she does not commit suicide. She does not sink unprotected into destitution and slavery, like women from the defeated side in ancient war. She is not silenced – as her final triumphant speech from the chariot shows. She takes over Jason's male responsibility of ensuring proper burial and founds an annual sacrifice to expiate the deaths. The effect of her usurpation of his role is in one sense to negate conventional ritual and to deny Jason the consoling funeral which would be the culturally expected culmination to his lament for his sons. Medea then embarks on the next phase of her life. Her words and actions display her intention to continue with her civic and family responsibilities, but bypass the fact that she was the agent who brought about the situation.

These different facets of Medea's behaviour – loyalty, energy, resourcefulness, vengefulness, cleverness, action and feeling on a grand scale – are heroic qualities introduced and developed at different stages in the play, often in interplay with perceptions of Medea by the other characters. Some critics have suggested that Medea's self is split between a feminine loving self and a heroic avenging self, which becomes dominant in the course of her anguished speech when she sends the children indoors (at lines 1049ff.). The article by Williamson, which you have just studied, analysed in detail the way in which Medea's dislocation is not just social but also verbal, physical and psychological. It is perhaps the suffering which she endures and displays in this last encounter which prevents her final escape being perceived either as an unmitigated triumph or as a moral disaster, although her heroic concern for *eukleia* (a lastingly glorious reputation) persists. Ultimately, 'how can she then survive?' is an unanswerable question. She does because in the myth she does and because the assertive heroic aspects of her personality have overcome the compliant aspects. AC10 considered the way in which the dramatist's language explores this conflict. If you have not already done so, you should also read the article by P.E. Easterling, 'The infanticide in Euripides' *Medea*, *Resource Book 3*, D10.

## Why audiences are so disturbed by this play

The two threads of the play that I have discussed are richly varied in their exploration of different kinds of relationship and in the range of civic and heroic language with which Euripides plays. In speaking and acting on her own behalf, unmediated by male relatives speaking and acting for her, Medea steps outside the patriarchal structures which limited women's freedom, yet in so doing she also suppresses the loving side of her personality. Thus Euripides lays bare the logical but disturbing consequences of adherence to civic and heroic values. It is hard to convey this awful irony when transplanting the play to a completely modern production context.

Medea is famous as a paradigm of the transgressive woman – in the wrong place at the wrong time, resisting wrong things but in the wrong way, challenging the boundaries which limit people who are outsiders but destroying the community she joined. What is important about her speech to the women of Corinth, coming as it does near the beginning of the play, is that it shows Medea as having an excellent understanding of the fifth-century *polis* community and its values. Recent criticism has tended to emphasize that she is a barbarian, that she is 'Other'. Of course this is important, but Euripides' glorious and frightening irony is that he represents her for a major part of the play as thinking, talking and acting like a Greek. In form and language the speech to the women of Corinth is an example of carefully crafted fifth-century political rhetoric. What is odd about it is that it is spoken by a woman on behalf of women, all women. To deliver it, Medea moves outside the house to a public stage and lays claim to speak and act as her male relatives could have done on her behalf. Thus, ironically, her eventual tragic actions are explained by precisely those values which she appears to transgress. I suggest that this aspect makes the play *even more shocking* for an ancient audience than for a modern one. Both ancient and modern audiences can relate to the strand of the play which reveals Medea as threatened by madness, but to suggest, as other strands in the play do, that Medea's actions in some sense *conform* to the implications of the civic as well as the heroic value systems is surely threatening to the ancient audience in a way for which it is hard to find a modern correspondence. No wonder the play did not win.

Please be sure to view TV21, which confronts many of the issues raised in these units.

# GLOSSARY

**agon** dramatic confrontation between two characters which consists of opposing speeches – a fighting dialogue or contest.

**antistrophe** see **strophe**.

**choregos** wealthy man who financed the selection and training of the Chorus as a public service or liturgy.

**Chorus** group of male singers and dancers who performed in the *orchestra* and who commented on the action of the play. In mid-fifth-century tragedy there were fifteen in the Chorus, an increase from the earlier number of twelve. The name Chorus is also given to the lyric or poetic sections of the play performed by the Chorus.

**dialogue** the formally structured exchange between two characters; in a Greek play it is often in the form of a dramatic confrontation, the *agon*.

*diegetic* **space** 'narrated' or 'reported' space for action which took place off-stage, imagined by the writer, actors and audience. To a Greek audience this was a 'real' part of the action.

**episode** the sequence in a Greek play between the Choruses where the dramatic action develops. Episodes have a number of formal elements, of which the most important are dialogue and *stichomythia*.

*exodos* the exit of the Chorus which marks the formal end of a play.

**liturgy** derived from the Greek for 'work for the people', liturgies were an important institution in democratic Athens. Wealthy men were required to finance and organize work in the public service. Liturgies might be of two main kinds: equipping a warship for a year or financing aspects of the public festivals. Provision of a Chorus comes into this second category. Undertaking a liturgy was a means of advertising a man's wealth (as well as redistributing it) and could also help him politically by boosting his reputation for wealth and public service.

*orchestra* large circular space in front of the stage where the Chorus performed.

*parodos* first or entry ode (song) performed by the Chorus.

*parodos/parodoi* the area on the sides between *theatron* and stage from where actors made their entrances and exits.

*polis* independent city state in classical Greece; it also refers to the public or civic arena, which was generally the domain of men.

*skene* the area behind the narrow stage where the actors performed; it served as a changing room and place for costumes and props. The front of the *skene* was used as a backdrop for the play, usually the façade and entrance of a house.

*stasimon* choral ode or song performed by the Chorus (apart from the first or entry ode, which is called the *parodos*).

*stichomythia* form of dialogue in which the actors speak one or two lines in turn. Repetition and echo of words are used for irony or rebuttal. It can be used to suggest conflict, excitement or to accelerate the pace of the action.

*strophe/antistrophe* two matching sections of choral odes and dances. *Strophe* is derived from the Greek word meaning turning, and indicates that this was sung as the Chorus turned dancing from right to left. The *antistrophe* accompanied the return of the Chorus from left to right.

*theatron* tiered seating in a concave semi-circle built into a hill where the audience sat.

*theologeion* literally, the place above the stage where the gods (*theoi*) appear. This was an elevated position achieved by the use of a crane, and was normally reserved for divine appearances.

# REFERENCES

LATTIMORE, R. (trans.) (1965) *The Odyssey*, New York, Harper & Row.

RECKFORD, K. (1968) 'Medea's first exit', *Transactions of the American Philological Association*, vol. 99, pp.329–59.

STUTTARD, D. (trans.) (1996) *Medea*, York, Actors of Dionysus Publications.

VELLACOTT, P. (trans.) (1963a) *Electra*, Harmondsworth, Penguin.

VELLACOTT, P. (trans.) (1963b) *Medea*, Harmondsworth, Penguin.

WARNER, R. (trans.) (1944) *Medea*, London, John Lane, The Bodley Head.

# SUGGESTIONS FOR FURTHER READING

If you would like to discover more about Greek drama, the best thing to do is to read more plays or see them in performance. You could start with *Electra*, another play by Euripides. This is included in your set book.

The following useful modern discussions of Greek drama are easily obtainable:

ARNOTT, P.D. (1989) *Public and Performance in the Greek Theatre*, London and New York, Routledge.

GREEN, J.R. (1994) *Theatre in Ancient Greek Society*, London and New York, Routledge.

GREEN, R. and HANDLEY, E. (1995) *Images of the Greek Theatre*, London, British Museum Press.

TAPLIN, O. (1978, rev. 1985), *Greek Tragedy in Action*, London and New York, Routledge.

WALTON, J.M. (2nd edn, 1996) *The Greek Sense of Theatre: tragedy reviewed*, London, Harwood Academic.

A useful collection of essays on representations of Medea is J.J. Clauss and S.I. Johnson (eds) (1997) *Medea: essays on Medea in myth, literature, philosophy and art*, Princeton University Press. In this volume the essay by Deborah Boedeker, 'Becoming Medea: assimilation in Euripides', examines the way in which the different kinds of language used to describe Medea point to the main dramatic turning points in the play.

A recent prose translation of the play is in John Davie (1996) *Euripides: Alcestis and other plays*, Harmondsworth, Penguin. This volume has a helpful introduction by Richard Rutherford.

You may find it interesting to look at one or more of the above, but they are all strictly optional for your work on A103.

# APPENDIX 1: THE MYTH

You should read this in conjunction with the first note on p.200 of the Penguin text, which gives the background story.

The story of Jason and the Argonauts (outlined in your text) is one of the oldest Greek stories, which (as a result of Greek exploration in the Black Sea area) may have developed into versions which are now extant. The outward journey is fairly uniformly told, but the return journey has a number of geographical variants, reflecting the geographical ideas of different periods and the desire to get the Argonauts into connection with various exotic places, including the North Sea, the Straits of Gibraltar, and even Africa. A particular detail illustrates the different emphasis which could be placed on the details of the story: the earliest version which we know (Homer, *Odyssey*, Book 12, lines 61–72) clearly refers to the 'wandering rocks' which clash together, crushing vessels which try to pass between as a hazard of the *return* journey through the Dardanelles, whereas Euripides (*Medea*, lines 1–3) lays emphasis on this danger as confronting Jason on the *outward* journey. In some versions the exotic detours on the return journey are interpreted as motivated by the desire to avoid a *second* encounter with the rocks. For significant variants in the later part of the story, such as the killing of Medea's children and Creon's family, see p.69 above.

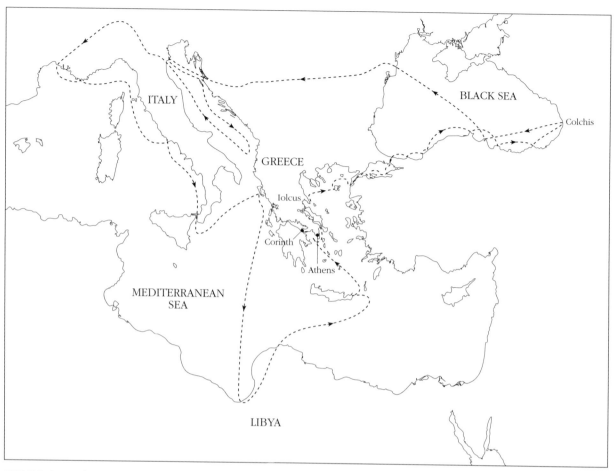

*FIGURE A.1 The voyage of the Argonauts (Apollonius of Rhodes, Jason and the Golden Fleece, trans. R. Hunter, Oxford University Press, 1993, map 1)*

# APPENDIX 2: EURIPIDES, LIFE AND WORKS

Euripides (*c*.485–*c*.406 BCE) was the youngest of the three writers of tragedy of whom we possess complete plays: the other two were Aeschylus (*c*.525–456 BCE) and Sophocles (*c*.496–406 BCE). Aeschylus was the author of the *Oresteia* trilogy, and you may be familiar with Sophocles as the author of the most famous version of the Oedipus story. Very little is known of Euripides' life; allegations of low social origins are part of the stock abuse dealt out by Aristophanes, the comic poet (*c*.457–385 BCE; see pp.93–5 above). What passes for his beliefs – his misogyny, his radical social and political views – is derived most probably from the content of his plays. It follows that, if we try to decide what Euripides' personal beliefs were, we will very quickly get into a circular argument: deducing his beliefs from the play and the meaning of the play from his beliefs.

His plays (about ninety in number, of which we have nineteen) were, like those of his contemporaries, based on the inherited tradition of myth and legend of the Greeks. As well as the Argonautic story, Euripides wrote plays on the story of the Greek war against Troy and its aftermath, including the murder of the homecoming commander, Agamemnon, by his wife Clytemnestra and the revenge murder of Clytemnestra by her son, Orestes. In comparison with his two fellow playwrights, Euripides' treatment of the legends, as in *Medea*, tended to be radical and subversive. For example, the *Trojan Women* focuses not on the male heroics and the Greek triumph, but upon the feelings, situation and treatment of the widowed Trojan female victims of the war. His plays appear to reflect radical cultural and philosophical beliefs found in other sources in the last quarter of the fifth century (see Aristophanes' satire, pp.93–5 above), possibly amounting to a 'radical dissent' from traditional belief. He later became notorious (though often on the basis of quotation out of context) for presenting his characters as questioning traditional views concerning morality, the gods and religion. You will be able to study further plays from Greek tragedy in the Open University's classical studies courses, for example, A209 *Fifth Century Athens: Democracy and City State*.

# APPENDIX 3: THE TEXT

The translation of *Medea* you are reading in this course is based on the 'Oxford Text', an internationally recognized edition of the Greek text. The path between Euripides' original and this, however, is a long and twisted one. We know nothing directly about Euripides' original manuscript; it would have been composed on papyrus, a writing material made from the papyrus plant found in Egypt and the standard medium for written texts until the early years of the Common Era. As papyrus is very friable in climates which contain moisture, writing in this medium tended not to survive physically for long, except from the dry sands of Egypt, which has proved a fertile source of texts, chiefly administrative documents and not, unfortunately, whole plays of Euripides! The plays which we do possess survived, like other Greek literature, through continual recopying, incorporation into libraries, and acceptance as 'school' texts (and many were lost, hence the small proportion of plays which survive), until they reached the stage of being copied onto a more durable material, parchment, in the early medieval period. The earliest texts of Euripides in this material which survive date from the later medieval period, having been copied out by Christian monks, and are known as 'manuscripts' (MSS). In the case of almost all ancient Greek literature (Euripides is no exception), for any work a number of MSS survive which contain divergent 'readings' at many points, representing mistakes in the copying process over the centuries, not to say millennia. By closely studying the errors, editors are able to sort out the MSS into 'families' and construct a 'family tree' – that is, show which MSS are more reliable and which depend upon which. The editor of the text on which your translation is based, by studying the different MSS and using accumulated knowledge of the language and society of fifth-century Athens, has 'established' what he/she thinks is most likely to be closest to the original of Euripides, using a specialist skill known as 'textual criticism'. So, what you are reading is a translation of a text which is the nearest modern scholarship thinks it can get to the original, given the inherent limitations of the task. It is still possible to disagree over details, and there are points – not many in *Medea* – known as 'cruxes' where the editor cannot be certain what the original text was: he/she has, in effect, 'given up'. But it is still theoretically possible, if not very likely, that valuable new evidence will turn up from Egypt!

# ACKNOWLEDGEMENTS

Grateful acknowledgement is made to the following source for permission to reproduce material in this unit:

Figure A.1: adapted from © Richard Hunter 1993. Reprinted from *Jason and the Golden Fleece (The Argonautica)*. Translated with an Introduction and Explanatory Notes by Richard Hunter (1993) by permission of Oxford University Press.

# UNIT 22 EXPRESSION AND REPRESENTATION IN MUSIC: RICHARD STRAUSS'S *DON JUAN*

*Written for the course team by Fiona Richards*

## Contents

| STUDY COMPONENTS | | | | |
|---|---|---|---|---|
| Weeks of study | Texts | TV | AC | Set books |
| 1 | *Illustration Book* | TV22 | AC10 (Side 2) AC11 | – |

## Aims and objectives

Although some weeks have passed since you listened to any music as part of A103, I hope that in the intervening period you have been more aware of the make-up of music – the ingredients and their effects. Music now reappears in Block 5, and we have placed it here for several reasons. First, you've just completed your work on two dramatic texts. In both *Pygmalion* and *Medea* you looked at the ways in which characters are depicted through dramatic dialogue; in Unit 22 you will see how composers have attempted to depict characters in music, and how music can be a 'representational art'. Second, the two plays are based on myths; your main case study in Unit 22, composer Richard Strauss's *Don Juan*, is based on a legendary figure. Third, there are parallels between Strauss's rethinking of traditional musical structures and Jean Rhys's rethinking of narrative structures in *Wide Sargasso Sea*, your text for Study Week 23.

The purpose of Study Week 22 is, therefore, both to build on the skills of musical analysis that you began in Unit 3 and to consider one main text, Richard Strauss's *Don Juan*, within an interdisciplinary block of study. By the end of this week, you should feel able to discuss some of the musical issues raised, and should be more familiar with some of the detail of *Don Juan*.

## How to plan your week

### Audio-cassette player

As in Study Week 3, this week's study will involve you in a mixture of activities, and you will again need to have a cassette player to hand. There are two audio-cassettes associated with this week's work – AC10 (Side 2 only) and AC11. As with Unit 3, set your tape-counter (if you have one) to zero at the beginning of each side of the cassette, and then write down in the unit the number that the counter reaches at the beginning of each subsequent item.

**Your study strategy**

During the course of this week you will revisit the elements of music that you met in Unit 3, but now you will focus on the ways in which composers manipulate these elements for specific purposes. You will also begin work on the question of how we, as listeners, interpret pieces of music, and you will be asked to read various musical criticisms.

Sections 1 and 2 introduce a number of musical extracts, and guide you through some of the broader questions that need to be considered before you go on, in Section 3, to look at the musical detail of your major work for study – *Don Juan*. Sections 1 and 2 are intended to take you about four hours, and don't involve repeated listening. Section 3 – the case study of *Don Juan* – involves close listening, and so suggested work pauses have been included. For all the listening exercises in the unit, try to ensure that you engage in 'active listening', as I recommended for Unit 3, and that – if possible – you will not be interrupted or distracted.

As you work through the unit, always try to bear in mind the themes of Block 5 – the reworking of a myth, representation of character, traditions and conventions, and issues of performance. TV22 helps you explore one of these themes – the reworking of myth – by examining composer Judith Weir's musical versions of a Scottish myth.

# 1 CAN MUSIC MEAN ANYTHING?

## An initial listening session

At the beginning of Unit 3 you were asked what music meant to you, and you were given a selection of writings – on the function of music – from some of the musicians encountered in A103. You may recall that these personal responses – from George Martin, Judith Weir, and so on – ranged from viewing music as an abstract, intangible art form to seeing it as capable of unlocking feelings and exciting passions.

This week you're going to take the issue of music and meaning a stage further. You're going to consider whether in fact music can be made to mean something specific, and we will look at the ways in which composers manipulate the elements of music for a particular expressive purpose. In Study Week 3 we touched on this subject with Mozart's aria 'Dove sono', which was an expression of longing and determination. This week you're going to look at how composers have attempted to *represent* something in musical terms, and in particular how places and characters may be depicted through the elements of music.

I'd like you to begin, however, by seeing how the listener might apply a meaning to a piece of music – even where it is not specified by the composer.

## CASSETTE 10, SIDE 2, ITEM 1

I'd like you to start by listening to a piece of music. Item 1 on AC10 (Side 2) is a piece for orchestra. Listen to the whole of this item, and write down your feelings about it. What is it about? What, if anything, is it saying to you? I don't want to give you any further directions at this stage: just listen and comment, drawing on your knowledge of the elements of music. (To remind yourself about these, you may like to re-read p.101 of Block 1 before you attempt this exercise.) Item 1 lasts for approximately nine minutes.

## DISCUSSION

Item 1 was the last movement of Beethoven's Symphony No.7 – a four-movement work for orchestra composed in 1811–12.

The **symphony** originated in the eighteenth century as a piece of abstract orchestral music, and became established as a large-scale work with no meaning other than a purely musical one. In other words, symphonies were not about anything other than their own musical components, or elements – and the way in which these were put together.

This is what you may have focused on in your own response to Item 1, and indeed Beethoven allocated no specific meaning to his Seventh Symphony. On the other hand you may have adopted a more interpretative approach. Writing in the nineteenth century, E.T.A. Hoffman advocated just this, proposing that the listener should find in Beethoven his or her own personal meaning.

FIGURE 22.1 *Ludwig van Beethoven (in Robbins Landon, 1970, p.313); collection H.C. Bodmer. (Reproduced by permission of the Beethoven-haus, Bonn)*

But what meanings might individuals look for? Both in his lifetime (1770–1827) and after his death, Beethoven was the focus of attention because of his nonconformist personality, his situation as a musician battling against deafness, and his position in the musical world as a composer of striking originality. As a result, the notion of 'Beethoven the hero and genius' has been a powerful symbol for subsequent composers and for political parties, with his music adopted by both left- and right-wing extremists. The Seventh Symphony has provoked a huge range of responses, with listeners over many years reading a variety of meanings into the music – even though, as I said, Beethoven did not give it any of these meanings himself.

For example, Robert Schumann – one of whose songs you heard in TV13, and whose flowery description of Franz Liszt as pianist you read in Unit 3 – saw in this movement a merry wedding, a heavenly bride with a rose in her hair. In contrast Leopold Hirschberg, a German propagandist during the First World War, argued that it was a celebratory work, written to commemorate a famous victory over France during the Napoleonic Wars (even though the particular victory he referred to did not take place until three years after the first performance of the symphony). This latter interpretation carried such weight that it continued to serve between the world wars, to the extent that the piece was perceived as a summons to the German nation and, during the Second World War, as a symbol of victory and power. And in 1989, at the dismantling of the Berlin Wall, the Berlin Philharmonic Orchestra performed this symphony in its entirety to celebrate the jubilance of the occasion.

Here are some of the responses to the fourth movement of the work:

### Ludwig Rellstab, journalist, 1828

Here reigns a colossal energy of the inventing spirit, which can hardly find satisfaction even in extreme measures. It is a chaos filled with cosmic thoughts in which we view with amazement the genius who created it, while at the same time we confess that the elements still appear too much in conflict for us to see the ordered world, founded on the standard and law of beauty.

*(quoted in Haskell, 1995, p.93)*

### Richard Wagner, composer, 1870

And with an Hungarian peasant's-dance he played (in the last movement of his A-major symphony) a tune to all nature, so that whoever should see her dancing to it might deem he saw a new planet arise before his very eyes in the prodigious circling vortex.

*(Wagner, 1903, p.66)*

**William Henderson, critic, 1915**

Music is the most complete and self-reliant of the arts. It has no utilitarian purpose, like architecture; it never, like literature, becomes a treasure chest for the archives of history. Despite Wagner's exhilarating interpretation of the Seventh Symphony as 'the apotheosis of the dance', that composition remains an absolute symphony in A major, capable of resting wholly upon its own musical beauty.

*(quoted in Haskell, p.237)*

**Olin Downes, critic, 1937**

To read events, for example as many people have, into Beethoven's Seventh Symphony is ... impertinent and beside the mark ...

*(quoted in Haskell, p.318)*

These four commentators, and the others I mentioned, vary widely in their interpretations of the work – ranging from viewing the piece as 'pure' music to imbuing it with specific, often extravagant and rather fanciful meaning. It is fascinating to witness these writers supplying their own meaning, even though Beethoven himself did not provide any clues. The main purpose of that initial exercise was to enable you both to form your own interpretation of a work and to observe interpretations by others. At the end of this week's study we shall return to the subject of criticism and the reception of pieces of music and their performances.

The next stage is to look at works in which the composer has actually attempted to convey something specific, whether a sentiment or an impression.

# 2  IS IT POSSIBLE TO REPRESENT SOMETHING IN MUSIC?

## Introduction

With the Beethoven extract in Item 1, you saw that a piece may have no specific intended meaning, but may come to be associated with one because of successive interpretations by listeners. However, it is also the case that composers have attempted to capture the essential elements of events, nature and characters in purely musical terms – to represent in sound such things as battles, water or the spirit of a particular place. In fact, although Beethoven did not depict anything in particular in his Seventh Symphony, he had previously introduced **extra-musical** elements (allusions to something outside the musical substance itself) in his Sixth Symphony (the 'Pastoral').

But how can a composer do this? Is it really possible for a composer to represent something 'extra-musical' in music by designing musical patterns that he or she feels come closest to the spirit of the 'thing'? Do you – the listener – need to know what the composer is trying to represent in order to recognize the intentions? For example, if we had a piece by a composer for which the title was lost, would we still be able to know exactly what it was about? Sometimes a composer may be deliberately vague with the choice of title. The French composer Claude Debussy wrote a series of short piano pieces in which the title was given only at the end of the piece, rather than at the beginning, and even then the title could be ambiguous. For example, one of his piano pieces is called *Voiles*, which can mean either 'sails' or 'veils'.

## Words and music: Kate Bush

Where words are involved as a starting-point, composers have something concrete to draw on – words that already have a meaning and that may be complemented musically. If you think back to the Mozart aria ('Dove sono') in Unit 3, you will recall that contrasting sentiments of regret and determination were matched respectively by slow, drooping music and a faster, more positive sound.

### CASSETTE 10, SIDE 2, ITEM 2

Listen to Item 2, a song by Kate Bush, the words of which are given below. How are these words complemented in the music?

**Rocket's Tail (For Rocket)**

That November night, looking up into the sky,
You said 'Hey, wish that was me up there –
It's the biggest rocket I could find
And it's holding the night in its arms
If only for a moment.
I can't see the look in its eyes
But I'm sure it must be laughing.'
But it seemed to me the saddest thing I'd ever seen
And I thought you were crazy wishing such a thing –

I saw only a stick on fire
Alone on its journey
Home to the quickening ground
With no one there to catch it.

I put on my pointed hat
And my black and silver suit
And I check my gunpowder pack
And I strap the stick on my back
And dressed as a rocket on Waterloo Bridge
Nobody seems to see me
Then with the fuse in my hand
And now shooting into the night
And still as a rocket
I land in the river.

Was it me said you were crazy?
I put on my cloudiest suit
Size 5 lightning boots too
'Coz I am a rocket
On fire
Look at me go with my tail on fire
With my tail on fire
On fire
Hey, look at me go, look at me ...
*(Kate Bush, 1989)*

## DISCUSSION

The song opens with voices only. The tempo is quite relaxed, and Kate Bush's voice ponders and reflects over a background of female voices (the Trio Bulgarka) singing harmonies. There is a **pulse** (beat), but this is not prominent, and at this stage the music feels quite fluid. After the words 'And now shooting into the night' the music changes. It is the action of the 'shooting into the night' that sparks off this change. Rhythm is now much more clearly defined and the band enters. From this point on there is a gradual build-up of sound to accompany the movement towards the rocket's explosion. From the words 'I put on my cloudiest suit', the voices are now only part of a much thicker, 'crazier' texture: the pulse becomes more dominant, and the mounting excitement in the words is matched by a 'take-off' in the music, building up to the rocket's 'whee' as it explodes. The song ends with the trailing-off of sound as the rocket falls from the sky.

FIGURE 22.2   *Kate Bush in performance, Hamburg, 1979. (Reproduced by permission of Redferns Music Picture Library)*

## Music without words

**EXERCISE**

As preparation for our study of *Don Juan* in Section 3, write down your thoughts about the following question:

*Many composers have used music to depict a scene or tell a story, even if – unlike Kate Bush – they have no words to draw upon. If a composer wants to do this, what are his/her means of doing so?*

Try to format your answer in continuous prose, and restrict yourself to 75–150 words. Doing this will help you develop a method of writing about music in preparation for the TMAs in the latter part of A103.

**DISCUSSION**

Music is sound: it can create a mood, but not necessarily one that can be defined. However, music *can* attempt to depict or narrate, as you will discover. I hope that this question prompted you to recall the first music unit, Unit 3, in which you were introduced to the elements of music. These elements are what the composer has at his or her command – namely rhythm, pitch, timbre and texture, combined within a form or structure.

For example, the composer can choose specific instruments for a particular effect, or can shape a melody according to a particular purpose. If you think back to Takemitsu's *Rain Tree* (TV3), you will recall that he selected the percussion sounds of marimba and vibraphone to capture the sound of delicate rain droplets; and Debussy's 'Jardins sous la pluie', which you heard some time ago in TV1, uses a light piano texture and rapid movement to impart the impression of rain.

### CASSETTE 10, SIDE 2, ITEM 3

Now listen to Item 3, a discussion of some of the ways in which composers have attempted to represent something in music. The means by which they have done this include selecting appropriate tempi (speeds), indicating suitable dynamics, choosing particular instruments and creating melodic and rhythmic shapes that they feel convey the spirit of the thing they are portraying. Listen to this item in conjunction with the following information about each of the nine pieces that you will hear:

## 1 Claude Debussy (1862–1918)

*La Mer* ('The sea'; 1903–5) is an orchestral work in three movements, each of which is intended to capture a different mood of the sea. The movements are called 'De l'aube à midi sur la mer' ('From dawn to noon on the sea'), 'Jeux de vagues' ('Game of the waves') and 'Dialogue du vent et de la mer' ('Conversation between the wind and the sea').

## 2 Bedrich Smetana (1824–84)

'Vltava' is one of six movements from Smetana's work *Má Vlast* ('My Fatherland'), composed *c*.1872–9. Each movement is a musical impression of Czech scenery and legends; 'Vltava' is the river that runs through Prague, and is represented as follows:

## 3 Franz Schubert (1797–1828)

Schubert wrote his song 'Gretchen am Spinnrade' ('Gretchen at the spinning-wheel') in 1814, using words from Goethe's story of Faust, who sells his soul to the devil. In 'Gretchen am Spinnrade', Faust's beloved, Gretchen, sits and spins, singing 'Meine Ruh' ist hin' ('My peace has gone'). Schubert imitates the turning of the spinning-wheel in the piano accompaniment:

## 4 John Adams (b.1947)

Adams was influenced by the musical techniques of the US **minimalists** (La Monte Young, Terry Riley, Steve Reich and Philip Glass). *Short Ride in a Fast Machine* (1986) is a celebratory work, written for the opening of the Great Woods Summer Festival in Mansfield, Massachusetts.

## 5 Johann Sebastian Bach (1685–1750)

J.S. Bach wrote extensively for the keyboard. Many of his works involve constant movement, and interplay between left and right hands.

## 6 Felix Mendelssohn (1809–47)

In 1842 Mendelssohn composed incidental music for Shakespeare's *A Midsummer Night's Dream*. He allocated appropriate musical **themes** to the various characters in the play. Thus Bottom, the ass, has a 'hee-haw' motif (a term you may recall from Unit 3 and its glossary):

## 7 Olivier Messiaen (1908–92)

From his youth Messiaen was interested in birdsong and spent much of his time notating the calls of different birds. Birdsong was the inspiration for a number of works, including *Oiseaux exotiques* ('Exotic birds'), written in 1955–6.

## 8 Benjamin Britten (1913–76)

Britten was among those responsible for reviving British opera in the twentieth century. One of his works was an adaptation of Shakespeare's *A Midsummer Night's Dream*. This opera was written in 1960 and, like Mendelssohn, Britten allocated different types of music to the different characters. The music that you hear, with its sliding string sounds (glissandos), evokes the magic wood.

## 9 Elvis Costello (b.1955)

The song 'Miss Macbeth' (1989) – from which the extract below is taken – uses a variety of instruments to enhance the words. Miss Macbeth is a witch who wears a fishbone slide in her cobweb tresses:

> Well we all should have known when the
>     children paraded
> They portrayed her in their fairytales, sprinkling
>     Deadly Nightshade
> And as they tormented her she rose to the bait
> Even a scapegoat must have someone to hate.
>
> And everyday she lives out another love song
> 'You're up there enjoying yourself, and I know
>     it's wrong'
> Well how can you miss what you've never
>     possessed
> Miss Macbeth, Miss Macbeth.
>
> *(Elvis Costello, 1988)*  ■

# Chinese music as programme music

The short musical extracts that you've just heard were examples of ways in which composers have attempted to use sound to capture the essence of mood, or of movement, or of character. Many composers have tried to take this a stage further by using music to tell a story. Such music, where the composer tries to paint a picture or tell a story, is known as **programme music** – a term that we will return to when we reach our main musical text, *Don Juan*.

Much traditional Chinese music is programmatic, and one of the most widely used instruments in such music is the p'i-p'a (see Plate 175 in the *Illustration Book*). The p'i-p'a is a four-stringed lute of ancient origins. The traditional Chinese lute, played some 3000 years ago, had four silk strings played with the fingernails, thirteen **frets** (strips of gut, bone, ivory, wood or other material placed across the **fingerboard**) and a round **resonator** (the main body of the instrument). In the fourth century CE a new type of lute was introduced from Central Asia. This had five strings played with a **plectrum** (a piece of material with which the strings are plucked), a pear-shaped resonator and a crooked neck. The modern Chinese p'i-p'a is a combination of the traditional lute and the lute from Central Asia. It has a straight neck and a pear-shaped resonator. It has four strings, played with false nails, as the silk strings have been replaced by nylon and metal strings. And it has twenty-five frets, including six large triangular frets made of jade.

Two distinct types of music exist for solo p'i-p'a – lyrical pieces and martial pieces. You're going to hear one of the martial pieces.

## CASSETTE 11, SIDE 1, ITEM 1

One of the most famous and most ancient of all Chinese pieces is *The Great Ambush*. This would traditionally have been learned by ear (like the Irish music that you heard in TV3), but during the Ming Dynasty (1368–1644) it began to be written down in a form of notation using numbers. The work tells the story of a famous battle between Liu Bang and Xiang Yu. After Liu Bang's victory, he went on to found the Han dynasty in 206 BCE.

Find AC11 and listen to Item 1, the complete work, to acclimatize your ears to its specific sounds; it lasts for about five minutes.

## DISCUSSION

While you were listening to this piece, you probably noticed that there were a number of different sounds drawn from the instrument. For example, there were both single notes and chords. There was rapid **strumming** (fast hand-movement across the strings), some strange, almost twanged notes, and abrupt dynamic contrasts. The performer was Li Lisha (*Illustration Book*, Plate 176), who studied at the Conservatory of China before coming to the UK to lead the London Chinese Orchestra.

## CASSETTE 11, SIDE 1, ITEM 2

Li Lisha is now going to talk you through the piece in more detail, explaining how the different effects are created, and what they are supposed to represent. The discussion is quite short, and so you might like to listen to it more than once. If you have time, after listening to her explanation, rewind the cassette to the beginning and listen again to Item 1.  ■

# Summary of the unit so far

The aim of Sections 1 and 2 has been to reacquaint you with the elements of music and to introduce you to ways in which composers have attempted to use these elements for a specific purpose – namely to represent an event, a character, a place and so on. In the rest of the unit we will build on this introductory work by focusing on one main text, Richard Strauss's *Don Juan* – which you will explore in some detail, in a manner similar to that employed with *Pygmalion* and *Medea*. Before you go on to this part of the unit, take a break and think over some of the points covered so far.

# 3 A CASE STUDY: *DON JUAN*

## Programme music in the nineteenth century

In Items 1 and 2 you heard an example of Chinese programme music. We turn now to a famous example of nineteenth-century programme music – Strauss's *Don Juan*. Composers in the nineteenth century were keen to expand the possibilities of expression by combining music with art or with literature. In particular, they wanted to explore the concept of narrative, which you've already encountered in Units 19–21.

In the latter part of the nineteenth century, feelings ran high on the subject of whether music could or could not suggest events or objects. Opposing musical camps formed, consisting of those who adhered to the theory that music was an **absolute**, pure art form, which could only have abstract qualities, and those who supported the notion that music could have a programme. The absolutists believed that music could mean nothing outside itself, and they held traditional composers such as Johannes Brahms in high esteem. The supporters of programme music venerated Liszt, Hector Berlioz and Strauss, figures who still arouse extremes of empathy or antipathy. (There isn't room to include musical extracts by all these composers, but if you wish to listen to examples by Brahms, Liszt and Berlioz, see 'Suggestions for further listening' on p.162.)

Liszt (1811–86) was fundamental to the creation of a new musical form, the **symphonic poem** – an orchestral work in a single movement, which had a programme. His original idea was to attempt to transpose a poem into music – to take a work already created in one art form and to express it in another art form. Strauss (1864–1949) was influenced by this, and by new directions taken by composers such as Berlioz and Richard Wagner. When Strauss turned to the symphonic poem, therefore, he used very wide-ranging subject-matter, drawing on Shakespeare, poetry, legends, philosophy and even his own life and experiences. He himself was of the opinion that if music was good, then it must mean something, and therefore it must be programme music. For Strauss, programme music was 'art', whereas absolute music was merely craft.

FIGURE 22.3 *Richard Strauss, Munich, 1888 (in Schuh, 1982, p.90). (Reproduced by permission of the Richard Strauss Institute, by courtesy of Dr Christian Strauss)*

FIGURE 22.4 *Pauline de Ahna, as Elisabeth in Wagner's opera* Tannhäuser, *Bayreuth, 1891 (in Schuh, 1982, p.221). (Reproduced by permission of the Richard Strauss Institute, by courtesy of Dr Christian Strauss)*

In 1887 Strauss met his future wife, the singer Pauline de Ahna (Figure 22.4). The effect on his music was immediate: his new-found passionate love affair found a musical outlet in his work *Don Juan*, written in 1888. For the subject-matter of this piece, Strauss decided to use the legend of the notorious womanizer, Don Juan. Don Juan Tenorio, of Seville, was an infamous seducer of beautiful women, and his name was synonymous with the dissolute lifestyle of a rake and libertine. The legend had previously inspired a number of literary and musical works, including Byron's epic poem *Don Juan*, Mozart's opera *Don Giovanni* (an extract from which is included on AC5), and works by Molière, Pushkin and Balzac. Don Juan was also to be used by Shaw in his play *Man and Superman*.

Of the many variants of the story, the version of this legend that Strauss chose to use was a play by the nineteenth-century German poet, Nikolaus Lenau. Lenau's interpretation suited Strauss's purpose well as it consisted of short, fragmented scenes that explored not only the story of Don Juan, but also the psychology of the character. Don Juan glorifies the experience of the moment of conquest above all else. Ultimately this leads to restlessness and discontent as the conquest itself becomes tedious to him. In Lenau's version of the legend, Don Juan indulges in depravity and dishonour before being killed in a duel. Strauss headed his musical score with three quotations from Lenau's work:

> Fain would I run the magic circle, immeasurably wide, of beautiful woman's manifold charms, in full tempest of enjoyment, to die of a kiss at the mouth of the last one. O my friend, would that I could fly through every place where beauty blossoms, fall on my knees before each one, and, were it but for a moment, conquer ...

> I shun satiety and the exhaustion of pleasure; I keep myself fresh in the service of beauty; and in offending the individual I rave for my devotion to her kind. The breath of a woman that is as the odour of spring today, may perhaps tomorrow oppress me like the air of a dungeon. When, in my changes, I travel with my love in the wide circle of beautiful women, my love is a different thing for each one; I build no temple out of ruins. Indeed, passion is always and only the new passion; it cannot be carried from this one to that; it must die here and spring anew there, and when it knows itself, then it knows nothing of repentance. As each beauty stands alone in the world, so stands the love which it prefers. Forth and away then, to triumphs ever new, so long as youth's fiery pulses race! ...

> It was a beautiful storm that urged me on; it has spent its rage, and silence now remains. A trance is upon every wish, every hope. Perhaps a thunderbolt from the heights which I condemned struck fatally at my power of love, and suddenly my world became a desert and darkened. And perhaps not; the fuel is all consumed and the hearth is cold and dark.

*(Del Mar, 1962, pp.67–8, footnotes 10–12)*

These three quotations do not so much tell the story of Don Juan as reveal his character – and Strauss's work attempts to combine the characteristics of Don Juan the man with the story of some of his exploits. In order to tell the story in music, Strauss had to find a structure, and this he found to be a problem. In August 1888 he wrote to the conductor Hans von Bülow:

> I have found myself trapped in a steadily growing antithesis between the musical-cum-poetic content that I have wanted to communicate and the form of the ternary [three-part] sonata-movement which we have inherited from the classics ... I consider it a legitimate artistic method to create an appropriate new form for each new subject ...

> *(quoted in Schuh, 1982, p.146)*

What Strauss was saying was that the traditional **sonata form**, which he had inherited from his predecessors such as Beethoven, was not necessarily appropriate for his particular purpose. His aim was therefore to create a suitable structure that could combine a literary programme with some of the traditional musical principles of presenting themes and developing them within some sort of modified sonata form. Sonata form was the dominant structure used in the symphony and consisted of a basic principle that has some similarities with the dramatic structure you encountered in *Pygmalion*. Sonata form consists of the exposition (presentation), development, and recapitulation (bringing back) of musical themes. You may recall that, when you looked at *Pygmalion*, you saw an example of a dramatic structure beginning with an exposition (presentation of characters), followed by a development, middle, turning-point and climax. Musical sonata form begins in a similar way, but whereas the dramatic structure is linear, leading to a final climax, sonata form is circular, bringing back the main themes in the recapitulation. The challenge for Strauss was to find a way of utilizing what had proved to be an extremely successful and useful method of constructing a piece of music, while freeing it up so that it could also embrace extra-musical ideas. We will return to this issue later in the unit.

## CASSETTE 11, SIDE 1, ITEM 3

Before we move on to study *Don Juan* in detail, I'd like you to listen to the whole piece, Item 3. It lasts for about eighteen minutes, so allow yourself some uninterrupted time. I'm not giving specific listening guidelines, except to say that you might try to listen out for repeated tunes. After that, you might wish to take a study-break. ■

## Strauss's orchestra

You've now heard the whole piece, and – following the way in which you studied *Medea* – I'm going to take you through it, section by section. We're going to look at it as a programmatic work, seeing how Strauss depicts characters and events in musical terms. For *Don Juan*, Strauss used a large-scale symphony orchestra consisting of the instruments listed overleaf (Table 1) – some of which can be seen in Plate 23 in the *Illustration Book*. His decision to use a large orchestra with a wide range of instruments gave him the scope to select different timbres for different effects.

TABLE 1 *The orchestra for* Don Juan

| Strings* | Woodwind | Brass | Percussion |
|---|---|---|---|
| First violins | 3 flutes† | 4 French horns | 3 timpani |
| Second violins | 2 oboes and a | 3 trumpets | Triangle |
| Violas | cor anglais | 3 trombones | Cymbals |
| Cellos | 2 clarinets | Tuba | Glockenspiel |
| Double basses | 2 bassoons and | | |
| Harp | a contrabassoon | | |
| * numbers unspecified | † with one performer also playing a piccolo | | |

# The opening of the work

You may have noticed from your initial listening that there are recognizable tunes that recur at various points in the piece. These tunes, or themes, are the main musical elements from which the piece is constructed. They are also tunes allotted to characters. Appendix 1 shows you the musical notation of these themes. I shall discuss them at some length, and will ask you to refer to this appendix from time to time. If you find the musical notation of the themes difficult to follow, don't worry: the notation is in no way crucial to your understanding of the piece.

## CASSETTE 11, SIDE 2, ITEM 4

Now turn to Side 2 of the cassette. All the items (Items 4–22) are quite short, and close together because of space limitations on this side of the cassette. Listen to Item 4, the opening section of the piece, and answer the following question:

*How does the music make an immediate impact on the listener?*

Write your answer in continuous prose, and focus in particular on tempo and on timbre.

## DISCUSSION

This is an instantly arresting opening, almost a call to attention. Strauss uses the whole orchestra in a huge 'whoosh' of sound, indicating to the players that they should play *ff*, or 'very loud'. The overall feeling is of propulsion – with fast, chattering woodwind, blazing brass, soaring strings and driving percussion. At the very beginning of the passage, the music played by the higher instruments, such as violins and flutes, moves upwards, while that of the lower instruments, such as trombones and double basses, moves downwards, so that the effect created is that of a rapid opening out of sound. The impression is one of power and vigour, with driving rhythms and dense, busy textures.

---

This opening, virile 'swagger' is an aspect of Don Juan's character, and also emblematic of the young Strauss himself (rather as Professor Higgins was emblematic of Shaw). Part of the Romantic image of the composer was as hero, with Beethoven being the most famous example, and Strauss was inclined to fashion himself in this role, making himself the hero of his own piece in a later work, *Ein Heldenleben* ('A hero's life'), and hinting at himself as hero in *Don Juan*.

## CASSETTE 11, SIDE 2, ITEM 5

This opening is in fact the first of the themes - Theme A. This is one of the main themes of the work, and returns throughout the piece as a symbol of Don Juan's exuberance. In Item 5 it is played on the piano so that you can hear the melody clearly. Listen twice to this item to acquaint yourself with Theme A, which you will meet again. If you find it useful, follow the music in Appendix 1, (p.163) but do not worry if you cannot read music. ■

# A flirtation

## CASSETTE 11, SIDE 2, ITEM 6

Listen now to Item 6 and answer the following:

In this passage, is it still possible to hear Don Juan's exuberant swagger? Do you also hear something else? A change of mood?

## DISCUSSION

You can still hear Don Juan's swagger rumbling away: the character is still present, and dominant, and indeed opens this section. But there is something new. There's a different, contrasting mood inserted into the buoyant music: slower, gentler, quieter music – with a thinner texture and a new theme – comes in, or interjects.

## CASSETTE 11, SIDE 2, ITEM 7

Now listen to this new theme, shown as Theme B in Appendix 1, played on the piano as Item 7. As you can see from the appendix, Strauss marked this theme *flebile*, which means 'plaintive'.

## DISCUSSION

Some commentators have viewed this section as a brief flirtation on the part of Don Juan, with Theme B representing the first, and most fleeting, of his lovers. This raises the issue of whether music is (or has become) 'gendered'. Is some music 'masculine' and some 'feminine'? In the nineteenth century in particular, many people held this view. Music that used a fast tempo, that had driving upward movement, and that was assertive and loud with decisive, sturdy rhythms, was seen as 'masculine'. As you've already heard, Don Juan's first theme (A) bears the hallmarks of these nineteenth-century 'masculine' musical characteristics, in that it is fast, driving and rhythmically strong.

The 'feminine' was represented by slow, gentle, drooping music of a looser and less rigid nature, often using 'feminine-sounding' instruments such as the violin, the flute or the oboe. The new, delicately flirtatious Theme B – with its quieter dynamics and thinner textures – accords with some of these 'appropriate' nineteenth-century female characteristics. Theme B doesn't last long. As you heard in Item 6, this section of the piece finishes with light, chattering violins, violas and flutes which lead Don Juan away from this brief flirtation.

In our exploration of whether some music was considered 'masculine' and some 'feminine', we need to take account of the fact that certain instruments had specific associations. Brass instruments, for example, had traditional hunting associations and were seen as 'masculine'. The French horn, in particular, had hunting connections, and its origins were the basic hunting horn made, literally, from bone or horn. This developed into a simple, straight brass instrument used in the hunt to signal the stag at bay and the calling of hounds. The next stage was a simple hoop-like brass instrument, and then a coiled horn that became the French horn as we know it today (Figure 22.6).

FIGURE 22.5 *Jean Baptiste Oudry (1686–1755), Hunt in the Forest of Compiègne (in Grove: Sadie (ed.), 1980a, p.704). Note the large circular horn, as used in the hunts of Louis XV. (Reproduced by permission of Giraudon/Réunion des Musées Nationaux)*

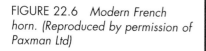

FIGURE 22.6 *Modern French horn. (Reproduced by permission of Paxman Ltd)*

To illustrate these points about the horns, we are now going to switch our attention briefly from Strauss and *Don Juan*. Item 8 is an example of a hunting song from Carl Weber's opera *Der Freischütz*, written in 1821. In this song, where the French horns dominate the orchestral texture, the Chorus of Huntsmen sing of the pleasure that hunting gives them. To hunt is a 'real man's desire', a desire that is matched with the 'male' timbre of French horns. Note the reference to Diana, goddess of hunting:

Was gleicht wohl auf Erden dem Jägervergnügen?
Wem sprudelt der Becher des Lebens so reich?
Beim Klange der Hörner im Grünen zu liegen,
Den Hirsch zu verfolgen durch Dickicht und Teich,
Ist fürstliche Freude, ist männlich Verlangen,
Erstarket die Glieder und würzet das Mahl.
Wenn Wälder und Felsen uns hallend umfangen,
Tönt freier und freud'ger der volle Pokal!
Jo ho! Tralalalala!

Diana ist kundig, die Nacht zu erhellen,
Wie labend am Tage ihr Dunkel uns kühlt.
Den blutigen Wolf und den Eber zu fällen,
Der gierig die grünenden Saaten durchwühlt,
Ist fürstliche Freude, ist männlich Verlangen,
Erstarket die Glieder und würzet das Mahl.
Wenn Wälder und Felsen uns hallend umfangen,
Tönt freier und freud'ger der volle Pokal!
Jo ho! Tralalalala!

*What pleasure on earth can compare with the hunter's?*
*Whose cup of life sparkles so richly?*
*To lie in the verdure while the horns sound,*
*To follow the stag through thicket and pond,*
*Is joy for a prince, is a real man's desire,*
*It strengthens your limbs and spices your food.*
*When woods and rocks resound all around us,*
*A full goblet sings a freer and happier song!*
*Yo ho! Tralalalala!*

*Diana is present to brighten the night,*
*Her darkness cools us like any refreshment in the day.*
*To fell the bloody wolf, and the boar*
*Who greedily roots through the green crops,*
*Is joy for a prince, is a real man's desire,*
*It strengthens your limbs and spices your food.*
*When woods and rocks resound all around us,*
*A full goblet sings a freer and happier song!*
*Yo ho! Tralalalala!* ■

Strauss took up and made use of these 'masculine' associations of the French horn, as you will discover later with Theme E – the second theme allocated to Don Juan, and this time played by four French horns. But that would be to jump ahead in our exploration of the piece, and we will now return to pick up the thread of *Don Juan* at the point where we left it – with Theme B just ending.

## Another love affair

If Theme B represented a brief flirtation, then the next section of the piece, with its complete change of scene, represents a love affair of much greater significance. This time I'm going to use the cassette to talk you through extracts from the piece, explaining how Strauss is manipulating the elements of music for a specific effect. Listen now to Item 9. You will also need to see Figure 22.7, which is referred to on the cassette as 'the figure in the unit', and Theme C in Appendix 1. You might like to listen to this item more than once – before taking another study-break. ■

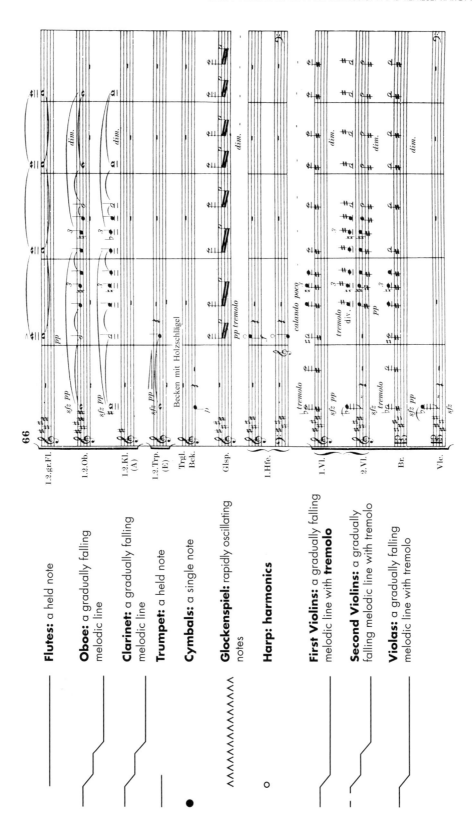

FIGURE 22.7  *Extract from the score of Don Juan, showing the quieter, slower sound world and more transparent texture*

# Transition and development

The next section of the work is a complex section of developing ideas. As there are a number of interesting musical features in this passage, I've broken it down into small sections. You will be asked a question about each small section as we gradually piece together the development of this section of the work.

## CASSETTE 11, SIDE 2, ITEM 10

Listen to Item 10, which is a variant of one of the themes that you've already heard. Which one is it – A, B or C? How is it different from when it first appeared?

### DISCUSSION

The first Don Juan theme returns here, but this time it's not so much a bold swagger as a rumble of discontent. You hear it quite fleetingly and it doesn't dominate the texture as it did first time round. This time, the theme is not played by the whole orchestra, but just by the cellos, followed by the clarinet.

## CASSETTE 11, SIDE 2, ITEM 11

Listen to Item 11 on the cassette. How is Don Juan's theme (Theme A) developed? Here you should be listening for ways in which the orchestral instruments share this theme, and noticing how it saturates the texture of the passage.

### DISCUSSION

The theme dominates the whole of this section. It's passed between strings, woodwind and brass and used in imitation (one group of instruments plays the theme, and it is then imitated by another group of instruments). The dynamics are loud throughout and there is a feeling of forward momentum with a series of rising musical motifs derived from Don Juan's theme. The orchestra then comes together with a loud upward movement.

## CASSETTE 11, SIDE 2, ITEM 12

With Item 12 there is a change of mood, and Don Juan's swagger theme virtually disappears. In this section, how does Strauss create the new effect of yearning intensity? The boxes in Figure 22.8 give you a choice of instruments and effects. Tick the three boxes that best describe Strauss's choice of colours and instrumental techniques.

Sighing clarinet motifs

Sighing flute motifs

Pulsing string chords;
tune in cello and viola parts

Pulsing brass chords;
tune in French horn part

Faint trombone interjections

Faint trumpet interjections

FIGURE 22.8

## DISCUSSION

The answer is that the new effect is created by sighing flute motifs and pulsing string chords, with a tune played by the cellos and violas, after which the texture becomes quite thin, with hints of Don Juan's theme heard as faint trumpet interjections. This is a sort of transition passage: it feels unsettled because you never really get to hear a tune in its entirety, and it's an intimation of yet another new section of music.

# A deeper love experience

## CASSETTE 11, SIDE 2, ITEM 13

The central section of *Don Juan* introduces another new melodic idea, Theme D (the first part of which is shown in Appendix 1). This theme is played by the oboe, an instrument traditionally considered 'feminine'. For Item 13 we have isolated this oboe solo to help you identify it; listen to it now.

## CASSETTE 11, SIDE 2, ITEM 14

Theme D is intended to represent the most important and most extended love affair on the part of Don Juan; it can be seen as a 'deeper love experience'. In the piece itself, the soaring oboe melody stands out as the orchestral accompaniment is kept to a minimum. This section then unfolds and eventually fades with quiet woodwind and violins. Listen to it now. I will not discuss this section but will leave it for tutorials.   ■

FIGURE 22.9   *Johann Zoffany? (1733–1810), The Oboe-player, c.1780 (in Grove: Sadie (ed.), 1980b, p.469). (Reproduced by permission of Smith College Museum of Art, Northampton, Massachusetts)*

## Heroic Don Juan

So far you've heard the three 'female' melodic ideas. These were:

1    the delicate, rather plaintive and fleeting Theme B

2    Theme C (the violin tune)

3    the oboe solo that you've just been listening to – Theme D.

You should also now be reasonably familiar with Theme A, Don Juan's swagger. The next section of the piece introduces another new theme.

## CASSETTE 11, SIDE 2, ITEM 15

In Item 15 you hear this new theme (Theme E, the first part of which is shown in Appendix 1). From what you've already been told about the representation of gender in music in the nineteenth century, how can you tell that this is a male character (in fact, another side to Don Juan)?

## DISCUSSION

Firstly, it's a French horn that plays this tune. (In fact, when you hear it played in the orchestra, it's four French horns in unison.) You may recall that brass instruments, and in particular the French horn, were traditionally 'male' instruments, and so this theme accords with nineteenth-century conventions. In addition, as you can see in Appendix 1, the dynamic marking is $f$ ('loud'), increasing to $ff$ ('very loud'), and the tune is very bold, four-square and direct: Don Juan is now a heroic figure, as established by the big leap that opens this melody. The theme has none of the yearning, gentle qualities of the three female tunes you've heard.

(At this point I should emphasize that we are talking particularly about nineteenth-century gender conventions. The concept of 'masculine' and 'feminine' music – and whether such a distinction is valid – is something that you might like to consider further.)

## CASSETTE 11, SIDE 2, ITEM 16

You're going to listen to the part of *Don Juan* that includes Theme E. The now heroic Don Juan dominates this section, but you can also hear his original swagger (Theme A). I've included (Figure 22.10) part of the musical score of this section so that you can see the point at which Themes A and E are combined. It may help you to hear the important musical events in this passage if you listen to it following the list below:

1   The section starts with Don Juan's new horn theme over shimmering strings, with some loud, powerful chords coming in to create a surge in the sound.

2   You can then hear a quiet oboe melody – perhaps a brief reminder of the woman left behind by Don Juan.

3   Don Juan's horn theme reasserts itself, followed by his upward swagger. There is then a section where his two themes are combined, as marked on Figure 22.10. This comes near the end of Item 16. ■

FIGURE 22.10   *Bars 342–349 of* Don Juan *– the combination of Themes A and E*

# Carnival

The next section of the piece has generally come to be known as the Carnival Scene, although Strauss himself did not actually call it this, and the nearest parallel to this in Lenau's play is a Masked Ball. This passage does contain some new music, which has a new mood and direction.

## CASSETTE 11, SIDE 2, ITEM 17

This exercise involves you in some detailed listening work, with a particular focus on timbre. When you listen to Item 17, note the ways in which you think the atmosphere has changed. How is the effect of gaiety, and perhaps carnival, conveyed? Listen closely to the orchestral sounds in this section, concentrating on timbre.

## DISCUSSION

The main changes to the musical atmosphere are in terms of the texture and the timbres used. The texture is much lighter, with none of the powerful sounds of the full orchestra heard in some of the earlier passages in the work. Strings and high woodwind dominate, playing short, clipped notes. You can hear an occasional (muted) trumpet interjection and a glockenspiel (and you might notice that this plays a version of theme E). The overall mood is light, increasing in tension as the section becomes gradually louder.

# Further development

## CASSETTE 11, SIDE 2, ITEM 18

The next section is a further development of Don Juan's two themes – his swagger (Theme A) and his heroic theme (Theme E). You hear these two themes in combination, with the trumpet playing the heroic theme, and the brass instruments generally dominating this passage. Listen to it now.  ■

# Don Juan's lovers revisited

After the carnival and the exuberant combination of Don Juan's two main themes, the music comes to a sudden crashing halt. The texture again lightens considerably and we are given glimpses of Don Juan's three loves (Themes B, C and D).

## CASSETTE 11, SIDE 2, ITEM 19

The three female themes all return in this passage, albeit in truncated versions. I'd like you to listen to the passage, Item 19, and identify the order in which Themes B–D return. Figure 22.11 gives you a choice of five orders. Tick the one box that you think shows the correct order (the answer is at the back of the unit). Before you attempt this exercise, it might be worth reacquainting yourself with these themes by looking at them in Appendix 1.

| | | | | |
|---|---|---|---|---|
| Theme B | Theme C | Theme D | | ☐ |
| Theme B | Theme D | Theme C | | ☐ |
| Theme C | Theme D | Theme B | | ☐ |
| Theme B | Theme C | Theme D | Theme C | ☐ |
| Theme B | Theme C | Theme D | Theme B | ☐ |

FIGURE 22.11

## CASSETTE 11, SIDE 2, ITEM 20

Listen again to this passage, but now it is to be found as Item 20. In this item I identify each theme just before you hear it.   ■

# Recapitulation

You might think that Strauss would have found a way of finishing his piece immediately after revisiting the female characters in the story, but this is not the case.

## CASSETTE 11, SIDE 2, ITEM 21

In Item 21, what do you think is happening here in terms of characters? Have you heard this music before?

## DISCUSSION

What Strauss chooses to do at this point is to return to some of the earlier music. You have in fact heard this passage before, or at least a passage that uses very similar music. This section is what might be described as a recapitulation of Don Juan's swagger (the 'recapitulation' referred to on p.139). The music here is very similar to the music at the opening of the work, although instead of starting with a 'whoosh' of sound, hints of the swagger theme are played by the strings. This passage acts as a build-up to the real start of the recapitulation. You can hear this when the full orchestra play the same music which opened *Don Juan*. Once the full orchestra is playing, the music continues in the same way as the opening section of the piece, but after a while Don Juan's second horn theme (E) is also heard. The overall mood is of dominant, buoyant forcefulness. (Before you read on, you may wish to take a study-break at this point.)

## The death of Don Juan

### EXERCISE

The final bars of this work have provoked numerous and very varied responses, with some listeners assigning precise detail to the way in which Strauss portrays Don Juan's death. I'd like you to read some of these descriptions before you hear the music. Read the seven passages below – each by a different author – and then, *from these descriptions alone*, write down the single musical event that you think will symbolize the death of Don Juan:

1   The fatal sword-thrust, represented by a piercing **dissonant** high trumpet note, is famous.

2   A lightning harp-glissando, like the flash of a darting rapier; a sigh in an A-minor chord into which the *f* of the trumpets pierces like a thrust – and then a collapse. The tremolos of the string trickle down like dripping blood; there is a muffled, wailing chord, a last ebbing of blood – and all is over.

3   Then comes the duel, with the death scene ... There is a tremendous orchestral crash; there is a long and eloquent silence. A *pianissimo* chord in A minor is cut into by a piercingly dissonant trumpet F, and then there is a last sigh, a mourning dissonance and resolution (trombones) to E minor.

4   His death in a duel is easily recognized in the music.

5   The debauch closes in a manner indicating the hero's fate, and at last his end is announced by the trumpet.

6   A final elemental burst of passion stops abruptly before a long pause. The end is in dismal, dying harmonies – a mere dull sigh of emptiness, a void of joy and even of the solace of poignant grief.

7   [The two principal themes] combine and, after a mighty climax, sound out a short tragic coda.

*(quoted in Brown, 1987, pp.266–7)*

## DISCUSSION

Although these passages offer varying interpretations, the one sound that is offered by many of the writers as indicative of Don Juan's death is a trumpet cry.

### CASSETTE 11, SIDE 2, ITEM 22

Now listen to the last few bars. You will hear the strings first; after a few seconds, the trumpet enters with a somewhat jarring sound.    ■

# Drawing together the components

I've taken you through Strauss's *Don Juan* on the assumption that it is inherently programmatic. Although Strauss never gave his listeners a specific, detailed programme, he gave us sufficient clues – in the title, in the three Lenau quotations, and in the convention of using the French horn as a 'male' symbol – to allow us to interpret the piece in this way. And a number of his works that followed *Don Juan* were also intentionally programmatic. Whether it is possible to assign such precise meaning as I have done to the various sections of the piece is debatable, but it is certainly the case that music is being used here to represent something, and for a particular purpose.

### CASSETTE 11, SIDE 1, ITEM 3

I'd now like you to conclude your listening work by returning to *Side 1* of AC11 to find Item 3, the complete work. Listen to Strauss's *Don Juan* once more, using the grid in Figure 22.12 (overleaf). This chart shows you:

1   *Don Juan* in purely musical terms, as a symphonic movement, with the themes labelled A–E;

2   the work as a programmatic piece, indicated by the row labelled 'Characters and events'.

You can use this chart as you wish. You may like to follow the themes that we've studied during our close listening work, or you may decide to try to get an idea of the proportions of the work as a whole. Note, too, that the comments underneath Figure 22.12 tell you something about Strauss's use of sonata form. If you find this figure unhelpful, simply listen to the whole piece once more, but this time try to be aware of the different sections of the work and the different characteristics of these sections.    ■

| BARS | 1–40 | 41–65 | 66–152 | 153–196 | 197–306 | 307–350 | 351–381 | 382–423 | 424–456 | 457–473 | 474–585 | 586–end |
|---|---|---|---|---|---|---|---|---|---|---|---|---|
| STRUCTURE | EXPOSITION | | | | DEVELOPMENT | | | | | RECAPITULATION | | CODA |
| | First Subject | Transition | Second Subject | | Episode | Episode | Episode | | Transition | First Subject | | |
| THEMES | A | B / A | C | A | D / A | E / A | E | A / E | B/C/D | (A) | A / E | E |
| CHARACTERS AND EVENTS | Don Juan's swagger | Flirtation | Another love affair | Don Juan | A deeper love experience | Heroic Don Juan | Carnival | Don Juan | Lovers 1, 2 and 3 | | Don Juan's swagger | Death of Don Juan |

*As in Don Juan, sonata form traditionally falls into three clear sections – Exposition, Development and Recapitulation – with the Coda bringing the piece to a close. The principle is that, in the Exposition, there are two main themes – the First Subject and the Second Subject, which are contrasted in mood. In this case they are Theme A and Theme C. (Theme B is merely a transition between the two bigger themes.)*

So far Strauss has followed the conventions, but he breaks away from them in the Development section. In the Development section of a *conventional* sonata-form movement, the two main themes are 'developed', i.e. presented in different ways. This is where Strauss breaks the mould: he does use Theme A, but instead of reusing Theme C, he inserts three independent 'episodes' where new musical material is heard. (It's true that Theme C appears in the transition, but this is merely a fleeting reference.)

Strauss breaks the mould in another way: in a traditional sonata-form movement, the Recapitulation brings back the two main themes – the First Subject and the Second Subject. Here Strauss brings back only the First Subject and one of the themes from the Development.

In this figure I've included the bar numbers in case you have access to a musical score and wish to look at the division of the work.

FIGURE 22.12   *The structure of Don Juan, showing Strauss's use of sonata form*

# Strauss and his critics

In Unit 22 you've seen that the question of whether music can represent something specific is a very difficult one to answer. And as you saw on p.136, during the latter part of the nineteenth century tremendous controversy raged over this issue, with opposing camps formed. The first performance of *Don Juan*, on 11 November 1889, was a huge success, with Strauss writing:

> I felt really sorry for the poor horns and trumpets. They blew till they were quite blue in the face, it's such a strenuous business for them ... The sound was wonderful, with an immense glow and sumptuousness ...
>
> *(quoted in Schuh, 1982, p.183)*

One of Strauss's critics, Edward Hanslick, was unimpressed, being of the absolutist camp and therefore of the belief that music could only be a self-contained art. I'd like you to read Hanslick's criticism of *Don Juan*:

> We have had, at last, an opportunity to hear *Don Juan*. Not Mozart's – no, quite the contrary. The name of the composer is Richard Strauss. Described in general terms as a '**tone poem**', the work is closest in content and form to the symphonic poems of Liszt. The score is prefaced by a lengthy extract from Lenau's *Don Juan*. 'The charmed circle, the infinitely distant ... Of many kinds of beautiful, stimulating femininity ... I should like to traverse in a storm of pleasure', and so on. [This translation of Lenau's *Don Juan* is different from the one that you met on p.138.]
>
> That Strauss consciously cultivates the imitation of painting and poetry is demonstrated in his other symphonic poems. He has not, as yet, gone as far as a new English composer (Wadham Nicholl) who called his orchestral composition, *Hamlet*, a 'psychic sketch'! But the tendency is the same: to use purely instrumental music merely as a means of describing certain things; in short, not to make music, but to write poetry and to paint. Hector Berlioz is the common father of this ever-multiplying younger generation of tone poets. With Liszt and Wagner he makes up the triumvirate to which one may attribute essentially all that these youngsters can, and will, do. In the one-sided study of these three orchestral geniuses, the younger generation has developed a virtuosity in the creation of sound effects beyond which it is hardly possible to go. Colour is everything, musical thought nothing. What I said about Nicodé's *Das Meer* goes double for Richard Strauss: 'Virtuosity in orchestration has become a vampire sapping the creative power of our composers.'
>
> These outwardly brilliant compositions are nothing if not successful. I have seen Wagner disciples talking about the Strauss *Don Juan* with such enthusiasm that it seemed as though shivers of delight were running up and down their spines. Others have found the thing repulsive, and this sensation seems to me more likely to be the right one. This is no 'tone painting' but rather a tumult of brilliant daubs, a faltering tonal orgy, half bacchanale, half witches' sabbath.
>
> He who desires no more from an orchestral piece than that it transport him to the dissolute ecstasy of a Don Juan, panting for everything feminine, may

well find pleasure in this music, for with its exquisite skilfulness it achieves the desired objective in so far as it is musically attainable. The composer may thus be compared with a routined chemist who well understands how to mix all the elements of musical-sensual stimulation to produce a stupefying 'pleasure gas'. For my part I prefer, with all due homage to such chemical skill, not to be its victim; nor can I be, for such musical narcotics simply leave me cold. It's a pity that there is no 'free stage' for emancipated naturalism in instrumental music. That would be the fitting place for 'tone paintings' *à la* Richard Strauss.

We could almost wish that many more such tone paintings might be composed, simply to provide the *ne plus ultra* of false licentiousness and precipitate a reaction, a return to healthy, musical music. The tragedy is that most of our younger composers think in a foreign language (philosophy, poetry, painting) and then translate the thought into the mother tongue (music). People like Richard Strauss, moreover, translate badly, unintelligibly, tastelessly, with exaggeration. We are not so sanguine as to expect the reaction against this emancipated naturalism in instrumental music to come immediately – but come it must.

*(quoted in Pleasants, 1950, pp.291–2)*

Strauss himself conducted the first performance of the work, and indeed he went on to become a renowned interpreter both of his own music and that of Mozart. Although space doesn't allow for discussion of Strauss the conductor, I have included the details of his own recording of *Don Juan* on p.162; and if you do go on to listen to this performance, you will find that it is very different from the one we chose for AC11. You might like to finish your work on Strauss the musician by reading his somewhat tongue-in-cheek Ten Golden Rules for conducting, which he wrote for a young conductor in about 1922:

1   Remember that you are making music not to amuse yourself but to delight your audience.

2   You should not perspire when conducting: only the audience should get warm.

3   Conduct *Salome* and *Elektra* as if they were by Mendelssohn: Fairy Music.

4   Never look encouragingly at the brass, except with a short glance to give an important cue.

5   But never let the horns and woodwind out of your sight: if you can hear them at all they are still too strong.

6   If you think that the brass is not blowing hard enough, tone it down another shade or two.

7   It is not enough that you yourself should hear every word the soloist sings – you know it off by heart anyway: the audience must be able to follow without effort. If they do not understand the words they will go to sleep.

8   Always accompany a singer in such a way that he can sing without effort.

9   When you think you have reached the limits of prestissimo, double the pace.

10  If you follow these rules carefully you will, with your fine gifts and your great accomplishments, always be the darling of your listeners.

*(quoted in Amis and Rose, 1989, p.118)*

# 4 CONCLUSION AND SUMMARY

In Unit 22 you've worked on the subject of whether music can be used to represent something, and have studied one main text in some detail. *Don Juan* is a work that attempts to portray characters in music and to present them within a narrative structure – that is, a chain of events in which characters appear and interact. The main points you should take away from this unit are:

1   Strauss takes a well-known legend of an infamous womanizer and reworks it in musical terms.

2   In order to do this, he depicts characters using the elements of music. The musical themes are 'gendered' by his choice of timbre, pitch and rhythm.

3   To tell the story of Don Juan, Strauss uses a traditional musical structure (sonata form), but remoulds it to suit his purposes.

4   Criticism of – and writing about – a work can produce widely differing interpretations, even though each may be supported by a valid argument.

# GLOSSARY

**absolute (or abstract) music** music without direct reference to anything outside itself.

**dissonant** jarring, unpleasant sound – as opposed to 'consonant' (pleasant, relaxed). Definitions of what constitutes a consonance or a dissonance have varied historically.

**extra-musical** something 'extra' to the musical elements themselves (for example, references to events and objects outside the music).

**fingerboard** part of a string instrument against which the strings are stretched and depressed by the player.

**frets** strips of gut, bone, ivory, wood, metal or other material fixed on the **fingerboard** of guitars, lutes and viols. By pressing a finger against a fret, the player shortens the length of the string and alters the pitch.

**harmonics** pure sounds that are present when a string or an air-column vibrates.

**minimalist** 'minimal music' is the term used to describe the work of La Monte Young, Terry Riley, Steve Reich and Philip Glass – US composers who were the first to develop techniques of repetition and reduction of musical means in their music. In TV3 you heard an example of this, with Steve Reich's *Clapping Music*.

**plectrum** small piece of material (wood, metal or some other substance) used to pluck the strings of guitars, lutes, etc.

**programme music** term first used by Liszt to mean music of a descriptive or narrative nature. Music that is programmatic attempts to depict objects, characters or events.

**pulse** beat.

**resonator** main body of an instrument.

**sonata form** musical form in widespread use from the mid-eighteenth century, especially for large-scale instrumental works. Material is presented in the Exposition, then 'developed', then brought back in the Recapitulation. Figure 22.12 shows a modified version of sonata form.

**staccato** method of playing whereby the notes sound separate or detached.

**strumming** to strum is to brush the fingers lightly over the strings of a musical instrument.

**symphonic poem (also known as 'tone poem')** piece for orchestra which is based on a poem, story, painting or suchlike.

**symphony** a piece for orchestra; most commonly a large-scale orchestral work in several movements.

**theme** group of notes that constitute an important element in the construction of a piece.

**tone poem** see **symphonic poem**.

**tremolo** shaking, trembling; in string-playing, the rapid reiteration of a single note by the bow.

# REFERENCES

AMIS, J. and ROSE, M. (eds) (1989) *Words about Music: an anthology,* London, Faber and Faber.

BROWN, C. (1987) *Music and Literature: a comparison of the arts,* Hanover, New Hampshire, University Press of New England.

DEL MAR, N. (1962) *Richard Strauss: a critical commentary on his life and works,* vol.I, London, Barrie and Rockliff.

HASKELL, H. (ed.) (1995) *The Attentive Listener: three centuries of music criticism,* London, Faber and Faber.

PLEASANTS, H. (ed.) (1950) *Hanslick's Music Criticisms,* New York, Dover.

ROBBINS LANDON, H.C. (1970) *Beethoven,* London, Thames and Hudson.

SADIE, S. (ed.) (1980a) *The New Grove Dictionary of Music and Musicians,* vol.8, London, Macmillan.

SADIE, S. (ed.) (1980b) *The New Grove Dictionary of Music and Musicians,* vol.13, London, Macmillan.

SCHUH, W. (1982) *Richard Strauss: a chronicle of the early years, 1864–1898,* Cambridge, Cambridge University Press.

WAGNER, R. (1903) (trans. E. Dannreuther) *Beethoven,* London, Reeves.

# SUGGESTIONS FOR FURTHER LISTENING

**Adams** *Shaker Loops*

**Beethoven** Symphony No.6

**Berlioz** *Symphonie fantastique*

**Brahms** any of the four symphonies

**Liszt** works for orchestra: *Orpheus*

**Strauss** *Don Juan,* conducted by the composer (*Strauss conducts Strauss,* vol.2; Preiser 90216, 1995)

**Strauss** further examples of tone poems: *Tod und Verklärung, Don Quixote, Ein Heldenleben, Till Eulenspiegel*

# APPENDIX 1: MUSICAL THEMES IN *DON JUAN*

*Theme A    Note that 'Allegro molto con brio' means 'very lively with vigour'*

*Theme B    'flebile' means 'plaintive'*

Clarinet in A

*Theme C    'molto espress.' is a shortened form of 'molto espressivo', and means 'very expressive'*

*Theme D    'sehr getragen und ausdrucksvoll' means 'very stately and expressive'*

Horn in F

*Theme E* 'molto espress. e marc.', a shortened form of 'molto espressivo e marcato', means 'very expressive and marked'

# APPENDIX 2: BAR NUMBERS FOR THE *DON JUAN* SCORE (AC11, SIDE 2)

The following bar numbers come from the Eulenburg edition (No.440) of *Don Juan*. It is *entirely optional* whether you obtain this score. We have inserted this information for those students who wish to follow the score when listening to AC11, Side 2, but it is perfectly possible to carry out the cassette exercises without the score.

TABLE 2    *Bar numbers of the items on AC11, Side 2*

| | |
|---|---|
| Item 4 | Bars 1–36 |
| Item 5 | This is Don Juan's swagger. It can be seen in the score in bars 1–5 in the first violin part, and then in bars 9–12 in the second violin part. |
| Item 6 | Bars 37–62 |
| Item 7 | This is Theme B. It can be seen in the score in bars 44 (Violin I) and 45 (oboe). |
| Item 8 | (This is a hunting song from Carl Weber's opera *Der Freischütz*) |
| Item 9 | Bars 63–153. The discussion in Item 9 breaks this section down as follows: bars 63–66, 66–70, 71–87 and 88–153. |
| Item 10 | Bars 153–164 |
| Item 11 | Bars 165–196 |
| Item 12 | Bars 196–232 |
| Item 13 | This is Theme D. It can be seen in the score in bar 235 (oboe). |
| Item 14 | Bars 232–306 |
| Item 15 | This is Theme E. It can be seen in the score at bar 314 (horn) and 510 (horn). |
| Item 16 | Bars 306–350 |
| Item 17 | Bars 351–380 |
| Item 18 | Bars 381–424 |
| Item 19 | Bars 424–457 |
| Item 20 | (as Item 19) |
| Item 21 | Bars 458–585 |
| Item 22 | Bars 586–end |

# ANSWER TO THE EXERCISE ON ITEM 19

The answer is the fourth option: you heard the themes in the order B, C, D and then C again. Strauss brings back each of the female themes as a sort of reminder of Don Juan's love affairs. You hear the fleeting, flirtatious Theme B, followed by Theme C (played here by the bassoon and the cor anglais rather than by the violin). Theme D then appears, but this appearance is quite different from the original one: this time a violin, rather than an oboe, plays Theme D. Theme C then comes back, played by piccolo and clarinet, and then imitated by the other woodwind instruments. At the close of this section, you hear a faint hint that Don Juan is about to reappear as the horns play a quiet, but accented chord.

# ACKNOWLEDGEMENTS

Grateful acknowledgement is made to the following for permission to reproduce material in this unit:

**Text**

'Rocket's Tail': words and music by Kate Bush, © 1989 Kate Bush Music Ltd, London WC2H 0EA, reproduced by permission of International Music Publications Ltd;
'Miss Macbeth': D.P.A. MacManus, © 1988 Sideways Songs administered by Plangent Visions Music Ltd.

# UNIT 23
# JEAN RHYS: *WIDE SARGASSO SEA*

*Written for the Course Team by Cicely Palser Havely*

## Contents

STUDY WEEK TWENTY-THREE

| STUDY COMPONENTS | | | | |
|---|---|---|---|---|
| Weeks of study | Texts | TV | AC | Set books |
| 1 | | TV23 | | *Wide Sargasso Sea* |

## Aims

The aims of this unit are to:

1   continue your introduction to literature by showing you some aspects of the nature and forms of the novel;

2   help develop your skills in careful reading and analysis;

3   consider some ideas raised by *Wide Sargasso Sea* that relate to themes in this block and other parts of the course: in particular, the cultural, historical and personal context or circumstances in which a work of art is produced, artistic traditions, myth, race and gender.

## Study note: planning your study time

Section 2 provides a detailed guided study of Part One of the novel and this should take about one-third of your study time on this unit. The more independent reading of Parts Two and Three in Section 3 should take another third of your time and the discursive text in Sections 4 and 5 should occupy the remaining third. TV23, *Real and Imaginary Islands*, will mean more if you can complete your reading of the text before viewing.

# 1 INTRODUCTION

By now you've had plenty of experience of poring over a text, an artefact, a proposition or an idea for far longer than you (or I) probably would in the normal run of things. The intention is not to persuade you that everything in life has to be studied so painstakingly. Rather, we want to show you that a great many more things and issues than any of us has time for are worth studying and would yield more of interest if they were studied, and that by giving what we can the attention it deserves our general awareness will be enhanced. To study one novel (or play or song) is not just to know that instance well, but to understand all instances a little better.

What is a novel? E.M. Forster, author of *A Passage to India* (1924), defined the novel as 'a prose fiction of a certain length'. This does not get us very far, although no one else has done much better, partly because the 'classic' nineteenth-century novel tends to be the 'loose baggy monster' identified by the American novelist Henry James, author of *Portrait of a Lady* (1881). The novel is at the other end of the formal spectrum from the sonnet, but that does not mean that a successful novel is disorganized.

Jean Rhys's novel, *Wide Sargasso Sea* (1966), is in prose, although it is so criss-crossed with rich internal echoes that it often seems 'poetic'. It is fiction in that it is 'not true', although, as you will see, it sets out to question an earlier fiction. Its length is much shorter than most 'classic' novels. It is divided into three unequal parts and each part is divided into a succession of sections separated simply by blank spaces on the page. There are no chapters and no headings. This is no ordinary novel and its text deliberately disturbs from the first sentence on.

# 2 PART ONE OF THE NOVEL

We'll start with a detailed reading of the first part of *Wide Sargasso Sea*, which was inspired by Charlotte Brontë's novel *Jane Eyre* (1848). You may have read this Victorian classic, perhaps during the preparatory weeks, but you do not need to know it in detail. All you need to know is that Jane Eyre is a governess, who falls in love with her employer, Mr Rochester. Their marriage is prevented by the fact that Rochester has a mad wife, who is locked away in the attic of his house. Rochester was married in the West Indies as a young man, in an arrangement made by his father and brother for financial advantage. His wife is a Jamaican Creole, and *Wide Sargasso Sea* relates the story of this woman's life, as Rhys, who was herself a Creole from the West Indies, imagined it could have been. Significant factors in the relationship between the two novels are discussed in Angela Smith's Introduction to the Penguin edition of

*Wide Sargasso Sea* (pp.vii–xxiii), which you could glance at now. However, since this assumes a thorough knowledge of this novel, a close reading of it is best left until later in your study of the text.

## First impressions

**EXERCISE**

Read the opening short section of *Wide Sargasso Sea* ('They say when trouble comes ... mortal man', pp.5–6). The numbered 'Notes to the Text' start on page 138 and you will find it helpful to refer to these as you work through the text. Then turn to the 'General Notes' (p.131) and read the sections on 'Islands', 'Slavery' and 'Creole'. Then read the opening section of the novel again. What is your first – honest – impression? ■

We're going to spend a long time on these first two pages, and as a rule of thumb it's always a good idea to give your very best attention to the opening of a novel, even when it's not as difficult as this. *Pygmalion*, you'll remember, gave its audience a while to settle down, but they'd already paid for their seats. A novelist has to 'hook' the browsing reader with hardly more than the opening words. Yet when I first read this novel, a long time ago and without the aid of notes, I was bewildered by its opening. Now, with notes, and the longer explanatory sections, I wonder if you felt 'How could I have been expected to know all that without notes?' or 'Even with the notes I still don't know where I am'.

But what if 'not knowing where you are' is precisely the opening effect the author wished to create? Then your reading, far from being inadequate, would have been just right. If you are yourself from the Caribbean, or know the region and its history, then you might well have picked up all the references without the help of notes. However, Rhys could be confident that only a small percentage of her potential readers in Britain would have this knowledge, and that for most of her audience this plunge into a different world would be as baffling as her own introduction to grey and chilly England had been in 1907. Yet England was far more ignorant of Dominica, the Caribbean colony where she was born in 1890, than she had been of England – a factor that finds its reflections in this novel. If you think back to *Pygmalion* again, written only shortly after Rhys's arrival in England, you'll recall that George Bernard Shaw was able to assume that, for most of his London audience, their own city's poor would seem like foreigners, with their own strange language and customs. In 1966, when her novel was completed, Rhys was still able to count on the narrowness of Anglo-Saxon horizons, despite two world wars. On the other hand, it's partly the lure of the exotic references that makes us want to read on and solve the mystery. That, and the threat – or promise – of 'trouble' from the first line onwards.

## EXERCISE

Go through the passage again, making a mark every time you come across another hint of trouble.

## DISCUSSION

You might have wondered whether there was anything you could leave out. There's a whole condensed story hinted at in the marriage of 'my mother' and the disapproval of the 'Jamaican ladies' and 'road repairing ... a thing of the past'. Look at the sentence in parentheses at the end of the second paragraph. Then there's 'their' misfortunes: whose misfortunes and what are they? And the 'compensation' for which they'll have to wait 'for a long time' – longer than some can stand. There's another untold story behind Mr Luttrell's suicide, related in a single sentence as 'calm' as the evening it happened. Soon his house is said to be haunted, and the very mention of a haunted house stirs our apprehension. No one goes near the haunted house. 'And no one came near us', the dead man's neighbours and friends. Despite this isolation, the mother 'still planned and hoped', and puts on a brave face although the 'black people' jeer at her. Even when her horse is poisoned she cannot let 'the old time go' as Godfrey advises (whoever he is: like the equally unaccounted for Christophine, he speaks a different language). He takes a very grim view. Yet all this 'trouble' must produce ambivalent responses, mustn't it, because whereas the Emancipation Act meant 'waiting for ... compensation' to the planters, to their slaves it would have meant freedom.

---

Now, on a first reading, you probably didn't notice all these hints, but their effect is cumulative and subliminal and we register them partly because they belong to a range of signs and signals so familiar that we may not even recognize we know them. Even if you've never read a 'serious' novel in your life before, you're a cleverer reader than you think you are. Fairy-tales, ghost and horror stories, detective stories in whatever form (books, films, comic strips, tall stories, gossip) – every story that depends on suspense (and what kind of story does not, in some degree?) uses the devices that are used here: the hints of a dark past, promises of a probably thwarted future, significant clues and meaningful silences. We voluntarily endure suspense in fiction because we can expect the pleasures of explanation or at least resolution.

## EXERCISE

What did you notice about the language of the passage?

## DISCUSSION

The words themselves aren't specially difficult, are they? It's the sense of not having enough explanation that is troubling. I wonder if you considered whether the narrator (the 'I' telling the story) is causing that problem or shares it with you? If the latter, what kind of person sees the world as so confusing? The first of the 'Notes to the Text' (p.139) has told you that the narrator is called Antoinette, although you wouldn't necessarily have deduced her sex from the opening section of text alone. But I think you might have suspected that this was a child's-eye view, not just from the references to 'my mother', but from the relative simplicity of the vocabulary and the sheer absence of satisfactory explanations. Whether or not this is actually how a child might see its shattered world is a deep question, but the child's view is often *represented* by writers as a sequence of vivid flashes with little explanation or connection between them.

# Points of view

We saw in Block 1 in relation to the sonnet (Unit 2) and earlier in this block in relation to drama (Unit 19) how writers choose to abide by self-imposed limitations. In the novel, '**point of view**' is another such formal device. The author chooses to write his or her story from a certain limited perspective. Here, Rhys has chosen to tell this part of her story through the eyes of a young girl in nineteenth-century Jamaica. (The setting of Jamaica is a relic of *Jane Eyre*: it's where the mad wife comes from. But Rhys never went there, and the predominantly Catholic inhabitants of Dominica will tell you today that, despite the Protestant servants, the island in Part One of *Wide Sargasso Sea* is recognizably Dominica.) What the chosen character would not know or understand, the author leaves out. This is a way of involving the reader, but it also inevitably implies that this is only one way of seeing the events that are recounted.

The presence of a specific point of view is clear in any first-person story like this one (a story related in the first person using 'I'). Ways have to be found of communicating events in which the story-teller is not involved: here the child overhears the strangers gossiping. In novels where the first person is *not* used, and the point of view includes everything that needs to be known about the characters, the perspective is described as omniscient (all-knowing), because the author is treating the world described as if he or she were its creator or God.

## EXERCISE

Within the child's point of view here, other distinctive-sounding voices can be identified. How many can you spot and how would you describe them?

## DISCUSSION

We've already noted the Creole speech of Christophine and Godfrey, which is described in the 'General Notes' on pages 134–5. It is compressed and emphatic, and in Godfrey's case also marked by a religious **rhetoric**. It most strongly contrasts, not with the child narrator's account, but with the **idiom** of the other adult speakers. I wonder if you noticed how it's characterized by complaint and accusation?

---

If you can't 'place' dialogue it's worth reading it aloud, even 'performing' it with as much dramatic emphasis as you can. If you do this you will spot that the mother's 'marooned' is an extravagant wail and that her diatribe against the loyal Godfrey is unfair and racist. The little word 'they' is crucial ('"He knew what they were going to do"', p.6), in that it introduces the idea of opposition between 'us' and 'them'. It's used in the same way in the parenthesis near the bottom of page 5 – '(they notice clothes, they know about money)' – which is probably a quotation from 'grown-up' English speech. We noticed how the same anonymous pronoun ('they') was also used of the planters. It's a usage that is characteristic of gossip and suspicion, isn't it? Although the child-narrator's account is not judgemental, the contrasting adult speech registers *difference*, and the tensions and enmity between the Creole speakers and the English speakers is going to be a very important feature of the novel to come.

## EXERCISE

We're not at this point told that the child and her mother are white and Godfrey and Christophine black, although this is going to be made plain in the next section. Why do you think Rhys postponed this information?

## DISCUSSION

If you said 'because it's not that important to the child' you're registering the child's point of view. Good.

---

A reader may guess that Christophine and Godfrey are black because of the way they speak, but may be less certain about the mother's race because she's from Martinique. I suspect Rhys was playing a game here, because most of her white readers would assume that anyone who could be described as 'coming from' the West Indies would be black. To many British people, a white West Indian or white Creole seems almost a contradiction in terms. What the text leaves out is a common misunderstanding, which is that 'Creole' always means 'mixed race'. This is *not* the case. Like the mad wife in *Jane Eyre* and the mother and daughter in *Wide Sargasso Sea*, Rhys was a white Creole, although it's not 'whiteness' as such that's important in the novel but the *white characters' difference* as Creoles, not only from the majority of the local population (who were black), but also from other white people like the more recent settlers *and* the white populations in Europe (see the section on 'Creoles' in the 'General Notes', p.134). As a minority descendent of European traders/invaders, Rhys had felt herself doubly displaced. Although Rhys's father had migrated from Wales, her mother's family had lived for three generations in Dominica and her great-grandfather had been a slave-owner like Antoinette's father in the novel. The 300 people of British descent living on the island when Rhys grew up there might well have felt 'marooned' among 30,000 descendants of their ancestors' slaves, especially as the brief French colonization had left the island

FIGURE 23.1 *Jean Rhys.*
*(Photograph by courtesy of André Deutsch and Penguin Books)*

predominantly Catholic and French-speaking. However, don't forget that Rhys is the **author** of the novel; she is not the same as her imaginary **narrator**, the character who purports to be telling the story. Although she draws on her own background, the novel is not her autobiography.

## EXERCISE

Now read the second section ('She persuaded a Spanish Town doctor ... any more', pp.6–9) and the associated 'Notes to the Text' (p.134). Do you think the narrator has grown up a little here?   ■

We (the readers) seem to be less overwhelmed, as if we were no longer looking up at a totally bewildering adult world from knee-high: 'I was old enough to look after myself' (p.7). Like the garden, Antoinette is neglected, so she spends most of her time in the servants' quarters 'some way off' where Christophine's songs reflect her loneliness and rejection. Notice that we now know far more about Christophine than we know about 'my mother', whose very name we don't even know yet. Christophine is a more substantial presence in the text than 'my mother', perhaps because she is a more substantial presence in the child's life. Do you see how Rhys stops the story for a moment to tell us how Christophine is 'different' too, and 'not like the other women'? She is a black woman who terrifies other black women – unlike other former slaves who only terrify the white people. The writer has chosen to build up some parts of her **narrative** and leave others quite shadowy and elusive. The mother is not fully 'there' in the text, just as she's not 'there' for her daughter. Fear, loneliness, poverty and a damaged child have distracted her.

## EXERCISE

Antoinette feels but does not question her mother's rejection, but she does ask questions about Christophine. Why? What do her questions and their answers allow Rhys to include in her narrative?

## DISCUSSION

Do you remember what we said about 'point of view'? Rhys has set herself the problem of telling us all we need to know within a convincing rendition of a child's consciousness. So the child asking questions gives Rhys an opportunity to provide us with some essential exposition – a term you should remember from *Pygmalion* and *Don Juan*.

---

What we learn here is what we need to know about the poisonous legacy of slavery. Christophine was a 'wedding present' – that's shockingly casual, isn't it? The same kind of peevish, nasty racial

generalizations that we noticed in the first section recur here. '*They*
stayed*' (the slaves stayed after emancipation) only out of self-interest,
insists Antoinette's mother, but whether or not she's right, she has just
moaned that 'we would have died if she'd [Christophine had] turned
against us' (p.8). The former slaves may now be technically free, but their
former masters are now humiliatingly dependent. The mother's poverty
and isolation may be pitiable, but she is also a spoilt, selfish, self-
contradictory woman who cannot adjust to a new order.

I think it's in the descriptive passages such as the paragraph beginning
'Our garden was large and beautiful' (p.6) that we are most aware
(perhaps not consciously) that, although this story is supposedly being
told by a child, there's an adult author at work here, elaborating on
sensual memories. **Description** is a feature of sophisticated fiction which
some readers don't like because it seems to get in the way of the story.

## EXERCISE

Do you think this passage is redundant or surplus in any way? If not,
what does it add to the text at this point?

## DISCUSSION

Did you read the notes? This is not just decorative, is it? The biblical
reference is like an announcement of symbolic meanings in the
description to come. The contrast between fertility and decay
('overgrown ... dead flowers ... fresh living smell') and between natural
beauty and objects of fear (snakes and octopuses) is intense. This is a
land of extremes – unlike 'temperate' Britain, which prefers its paradises
to be more restrained. Would you agree that the last two sentences ('The
scent ... near it') imply that there's something frightening about this
excess, even to the child who lives there?

It isn't just the garden but the whole estate that's 'gone wild'. The over-
abundance described in the garden would be a calamity in the crop-
fields. Indeed, the whole community has 'gone wild'. Overgrown
plantations are a disaster for the planters, but the same fecundity of the
land is a bonus for the ex-slaves. 'Why should *anybody* work?' (p.6) asks
the child, when things grow so prolifically.

This is a question still shocking to those who think the value of work is
self-evident: we often label this attitude the 'Protestant work ethic'. Work
was the penalty that God imposed on Adam for disobedience ('In the
sweat of thy face shalt thou eat bread', Genesis 3:19), and throughout the
period of European expansion and beyond men and women raised in
this belief were shocked to discover that some inhabitants of very fertile
regions didn't need to sweat all that much to live. Did such communities

represent what a paradisal life might have been like had we not fallen? So were *black* people closer to paradise? The question suggested all kinds of disturbing possibilities and it is related to the pervasive racial slander that stereotypes black people as 'lazy'. This was still a fiercely debated topic in books widely read by West Indians when Rhys was a child, as the quotation below indicates.

> They live surrounded by most of the fruits which grew in Adam's paradise ... The curse is taken off from nature, and like Adam they are under covenant of innocence. Morals in the technical sense they have none ... They are naked and not ashamed ... In no part of the globe is there any peasantry whose every want is so completely satisfied as her majesty's subjects in the West Indian Islands. They have no aspirations to make them restless ... They have food for the picking up. Clothes they need not, and lodgings in such a climate need not be elaborate. They have perfect liberty, and are safe from dangers, to which if left to themselves they would be exposed, for the English rule prevents the strong from opposing the weak.
>
> *(James Froude,* The English in the West Indies, *1888, quoted in Gregg, 1995, pp.49–50)*

FIGURE 23.2  *The Yorkshire landscape of Charlotte Brontë's background was a world away from tropical luxuriance. Wheeldale Moor, North York Moors. (Photograph: J. Allan Cash)*

You can see how the argument that the black Caribbean 'peasantry' live in a kind of paradise (no work, no clothes, no ambitions) slides into a justification of colonial rule and hence an assumption of white racial superiority such as Antoinette's mother expresses.

### EXERCISE

Now read the next section ('These were all the people ... a very black look', pp.9–12) and the associated 'Notes to the Text' (p.139) and try to describe in a single sentence what this section is primarily about.

### DISCUSSION

Did you say that it was about how the narrator is jeered at by a little black girl and how Christophine sees she is frightened and helps her find a friend to play with, but how after a while the friend, Tia, takes her clothes and so when she returns home her mother is embarrassed in front of some strange visitors and as a result she gets a new dress (as does her mother) and her mother goes off with her new friends leaving her daughter lonelier than ever? Well, you'd have found it difficult to pack all that narrative into a neat sentence. The point of asking for a single sentence was to prompt you to analyse all these incidents and see how they contribute to a unified theme. If your sentence included words like 'loneliness', 'isolation' or 'relationships' you are well on the way to identifying what this section is 'about'. But it's difficult. My own shot was: 'This section shows that it is impossible for the narrator to have an equal relationship with a black girl, despite a need that is prompted by her alienation from her own kind' – which is far from brilliant. Indeed, it shows at a glance that Rhys is telling us things that are far too complex to be fitted into a single sentence.

Let's consider Tia. At one level this is the familiar playground tale of the lonely child's desperate bid for approval. The complicating factors are race and the inversion of status that emancipation has brought about. You'll have no trouble identifying the powerful phrases on page 10 that express the black people's contempt for the newly impoverished 'old time white people'.

### EXERCISE

But what do you make of Antoinette's attitude to the girl she calls her friend?

## DISCUSSION

It doesn't take much for the racist generalizations to surface. She calls Tia a 'cheating nigger' (p.9). These are the attitudes she's been raised with. Both children are locked into racism.

---

Although this is the one moment when Antoinette's submerged attitudes are verbalized, I wonder if you think that the text continually stereotypes Tia in less overt ways? She's attracted to glitter – well, maybe all children are. But we are told there's something peculiar about her eyes and she falls asleep the moment she has eaten. These – like an indisposition to work – are the commonplaces of prejudice. They suggest that Tia is *different.* Even where the difference tells us that Tia is more of a survivor ('fires always lit for her, sharp stones did not hurt her bare feet, I never saw her cry', p.9), there's a suggestion that being tougher and more natural also implies more primitive, less sensitive. What's more – oh horrors! – she doesn't wear underclothes: proof of unrespectability to the straitlaced English. (Remember Froude's 'naked and not ashamed ... peasantry', p.177 above.)

On the other hand, you could argue that rather than stereotyping the black child, these details convey the white child's lack of fitness for survival. She's trapped by the standards of her vanished prosperity and status. You don't have to make up your mind *between* these alternative readings – both are simultaneously valid. **Ambiguity** – something you should strive to avoid when writing an *essay* – can allow the novelist a beneficial kind of double vision.

Antoinette wears Tia's dress, and perhaps she gains an inkling of Tia's socially inferior experience when her mother's guests laugh at her. But of course it's only superficial: she can't get inside Tia's skin, and although her family is poor it is not so poor that new dresses can't be found somehow. The friendship she craves can never be a relation of equals. But there's no promise that the newcomers will befriend the child either. As Christophine says, 'Trouble walk in'. In her view, 'New ones worse than old ones' (p.11). But whereas Christophine is confident in all her dire pronouncements (you could say that there's not a trace of the slave in her demeanour), the child's sense of her predicament fluctuates wildly.

## Characterization and realism

Sometimes a novel (or film or play) is praised because its *characters* are so *realistic.* Let's pause and think about these terms. I don't know whether you've ever been asked to write a 'character study', but it would be tricky in Antoinette's case, because her character is so elusive. We might say that's because she's still a child and her character isn't formed yet, but what I want you to accept is that this quality is the product of

Rhys's way of writing rather than the character of someone who – after all – doesn't really exist except *through* that writing.

Repeat a hundred times if you need to: 'characters are not real; they're *made up*', and they are just as much artificial when they're made of words as when they're made of music, as in the case of *Don Juan*. However, we readers are often deceived. In the traditional forms of the novel, which developed during the nineteenth century and continue to flourish in the more popular and easily accessible areas of the genre today, the main characters are frequently introduced with a kind of pen portrait, which seems to describe a 'real' person, and fixes their appearance and personality. 'I knew my traveller, with his broad and jetty eyebrows, his square forehead, made squarer by the horizontal sweep of his black hair' could be the introductory description of a hundred romantic heroes, and we know, because we have unconsciously absorbed the convention, that his character will square (forgive the pun) with his appearance, which goes on to include a 'decisive nose'. This is *Jane Eyre's* sardonic, sexy Mr Rochester, and what is peculiar (when you come to think of it) about what is supposed to be a first impression is that it turns out to be so reliable. Brontë's world-view was very solid. So is Michael Crichton's and Joanna Trollope's, writers of 1990s bestsellers of adventure and romance, respectively. All of their writings (and that of many others in the same tradition) embody a probably unconscious belief that 'reality' can be set down solidly on the page. So successful is this illusion that most of us as readers sometimes fall for it too. We say that characters 'assume a life of their own' and even want to know what happens to them after the end of their story. Remember this distinction between 'elusive' and 'solid' characterizations because we shall return to it later.

Rhys thought that the account of the mad Creole in *Jane Eyre* was not true to life. So her own novel both testifies to the power of the realist illusion and implicitly criticizes it. Because her novel tells the other side of the story of Brontë's alien, crazed, silenced and incarcerated wife, Rhys chooses another kind of language and another way of telling. Rhys implicitly does not believe that characters can be summed up with that confident British certainty that rendered so many Victorian novelists unaware of the rest of the world and their dependence on it. Nothing is reliable in her story: 'It would change and go on changing' (p.13), as Antoinette says. Of course, Rhys is not the only novelist to express herself through uncertainties more in keeping with the unsettling course of the twentieth century. D.H. Lawrence (1885–1930), for example, is often credited with being the first novelist to portray individuals as radically inconsistent and as behaving in reaction to their changing circumstances rather than on the basis of settled principles.

Paradoxically, of course, you could argue that to feel frightened one moment, safe the next and then anxious again for no particular reason (like Antoinette on pages 11–12) *is* realistic, especially in a child. But when realism is used as a technical term of a novel, we're not just talking about whether the story is convincing or not, but about a 'form' (far looser and baggier than the sonnet, but a 'form' nonetheless) capable of representing not just appearances but also ideas and values. Thus, Rhys not only uses language to evoke the sights and sounds of the West Indies, but explores the forces underneath the surface: conflicts of race and gender, economic struggle, growth and decay, sexual attraction and repulsion, religion and magic – to name but a few. You are not, at this stage of your literary studies, going to be asked to adjudicate on the 'realism' of this novel. But what you *must* take on board is that a novel is a construction, made out of words and fashioned by the writer. A character made out of words is no more flesh and blood than a portrait made out of paint.

## EXERCISE

The section ends with Antoinette even lonelier than she had been at the beginning. Reread its closing paragraphs on page 12 before reading on to the top of page 16 ('Angrily'). In this way you'll carry the sense of the child's sad isolation with you as you read short episodes that superficially seem to be about happier themes – love and romance – although discord erupts very quickly. Remember that every word counts; don't rush, and try to 'perform' all the different voices so that you can register their full and mostly unpleasant tones. Don't forget to read the 'Notes to the Text' on pages 139–40. There's also a section on 'Obeah' in the 'General Notes' on pages 135–7.  ■

I wonder if you noticed that, although the malicious gossip of the white community has been quoted extensively, we are not given access to the new servants' 'talk about Christophine and obeah' (p.14). Much as she wanted to be friends with Tia, and lonely though she is, Antoinette is far more closely in touch with the white community than she can be with the black, and the text unobtrusively records this.

To a lesser extent, her mother (and, we shall see, Aunt Cora) also inhabits the uncomfortable no-man's-land between the two groups. We've seen how Annette (she is given a name at last) despises her black servants, but at least she understands that they may have cause to hate, whereas her new husband admits 'I don't understand at all' (p.16). He infantalizes the black people (whom he would still call 'niggers'), interpreting what his wife sees as hostility as mere curiosity and their lack of enthusiasm for toil (which again we noticed was referred to earlier) as passivity: 'They're too damn lazy to be dangerous' (p.16). But Annette, who like her daughter ('She run wild', p.11) and the Coulibri estate (p.6) is 'wild' ('a little wild cat', p.15), maintains that far from being passive, the black people are 'more alive' (p.16) than her husband, whose language proclaims him to be a very cold fish indeed.

# Contrasts and emotions

The next two sections ('Mr Mason pulled ... in a looking-glass', pp.16–24) form the climax to the first part of the novel. This might make you think that here my questions and discussion will be stepped up even further – but no. If you have read as carefully as I have tried to persuade you to do, you're fully equipped to read and get the most out of what follows. Indeed, I'm sure words and phrases will leap off the page as themes we have already identified are developed in these crucial and – I hope you'll find – exciting sections. The pace can quicken because there is no need to pause for any but the most incidental exposition: the background to what is going to happen is all filled in.

### EXERCISE

If you have time, start the novel again from the beginning and read through up to page 24. In this way, you will see how your hard work has paid off. ■

These last sections are very *dramatic*, aren't they? You'll remember from the beginning of this block that while that term refers to the potentially theatrical or performable elements in a situation, it also implies vivid contrasts and heightened emotions. The first of the sections builds up the tension: the deserted village ('empty huts', p.16), the threatening sky and sea ('on fire', p.16), the spooky *glacis* (p.17) are the 'signs' (a word used earlier in this unit – see p.171) of more going on than meets the eye. The dialogue too is increasingly ominous, partly because Aunt Cora is so elliptical: 'Hearts have been broken ... children do hurt flies' (pp.17–18). Things have to remain unsaid (in case Myra reports them back to the other servants). What could be more of a contrast than the 'safe', alien, ultra-English trappings that the 'so without a doubt English' (p.18) Mr Mason has introduced?

Towards the end of this section (pp.18–19) the narrative drifts into what is sometimes called '**stream of consciousness**'. It forms an intimate extension of Antoinette's 'point of view', which imitates the child's wandering mind, instead of constructing 'proper' sentences. It also slows down the narrative pace, which makes the sudden awakening all the more startling and dramatic.

You know already that this is a text that makes little sense if you merely skim it. It's almost as packed as a sonnet. So to show you once more how much careful reading can reveal, I want you to try a two-part exercise.

### EXERCISE

First, what is Antoinette's reaction to the burning of her home? Just jot down your response from memory.

Then, go back through the last of the sections you have read (pp.19–24) and mark EVERY verb (word denoting action or response) that follows every use of the pronoun 'I'. (The first, five lines down, is 'I could *see*', the next, near the end of the paragraph, 'I *thought*'.) Then look over them all and try to characterize what kind of impression they add up to.

## DISCUSSION

I hope this has proved to you the difference between trusting impressions and relying on the text. My first impression was 'these events are terrifying, therefore she must be terrified'. But when I went back very much more methodically to the text and looked at the verbs that chart Antoinette's response, I found that terror was only a small part of it.

Few of the verbs that follow 'I' are out of the ordinary and many only have any emotional content because they are negative: could see ... thought ... came in ... (p.19) did not see ... did not see ... shut my eyes ... remember ... looked ... thought ... (p.20) was so shocked ... looked ... saw ... heard ... (p.21) could hardly see ... recognized no one ... could not hear ... was afraid ... shut my eyes and waited ... opened my eyes ... (p.22) began to cry ... hid my face ... could feel ... heard ... did not see ... (p.23) turned ... knew ... would never see ... (p.24). We'll leave the final paragraph for a moment. Do you see how this kind of scrutiny helps to pinpoint, define and analyse the effects of the text? Antoinette at first sees and hears (or doesn't see and doesn't hear) and only gradually begins to react and feel, and this creates a sense of her being present yet only partially involved – a development of the isolation we have previously traced. There are just a few emotional verbs, but even these are not very extreme. If Rhys's primary intention had been to suggest a child in terror there are plenty of more potent words she could have commanded. Ultimately, the effect of this restraint goes beyond terror because what is really chilling is that the child sees so much, knows what she does not see, and reacts so little.

The final paragraph starts with 'seeing' again: 'I saw Tia' (p.24), and *then* emotion erupts with the sudden rush of more insistent verbs – 'ran ... eaten ... slept ... bathed ... ran ... thought ... will live ... will be ... not to leave ... not to go'. But of course, just as in the earlier episode, Tia rejects her (as she must). Do you see how next the verbs revert to the seeing and not seeing we detected earlier? And that when she records that she did not feel the blow of the stone she is echoing that dreadful absence of feeling with which she witnessed all the earlier events of the night? It is Tia who cries. Then, as if for the first time, Antoinette's seeing acquires meaning: 'It was as if I saw myself. Like in a looking-glass.' You might have thought that the stone signifies the absolute divide between the white girl and the black, but the looking-glass says that they are identical as well as opposites.

*

The asterisk in the centre of the blank space in the text of the novel at this point indicates a gap of time, and our pace is going to change too.

Read straight through until the end of Part One. Make notes and/or mark words and phrases that strike you or echo topics we have previously raised. ■

Did you notice that when Annette cries '*Qui est là?*' she is echoing her poor burnt parrot? And that the song Antoinette prefers seems to be a former slave's song? I didn't for several readings and I'm sure there's plenty I still haven't noticed, but these again go to show how every word in this novel is there to work. I'm not from now on going to ask you to pore over the text in quite such detail, although it is what any tutor would expect you to do before venturing on an assignment, and what you should do when you find your sense of what is happening disagrees with mine. The commentary that follows is designed to help you see the shape and purpose of this section of the novel. Use the page references to read the quotes in context and to evaluate what I suggest.

The convent proves a respite – of sorts: 'my refuge, a place of sunshine and of death' (p.31). It's not so much faith that soothes Antoinette as the convent's rituals: not only prayers and embroidery and pretty tales of heaven, but the incessant grooming. These girls aren't being educated to be anything other than docile and graceful wives – lessons in which the La Plana sisters excel. The fate of Antoinette's dead/alive mother seems almost painlessly to be absorbed into this passionless atmosphere (p.31) where all the antagonisms between husband and wife, rich and poor, black and white are safely excluded. But Antoinette is perhaps less healed than temporarily sedated by this beautiful confinement and even so there are glimpses of her less compliant nature. She stitches her name in 'fire red' (p.29), is dissatisfied with the tepid saints' lives (p.30), and yearns briefly for happiness (p.32). But when moved to pray to be preserved from a desire for death, she stops praying and 'I felt bolder, happier, more free. But not so safe' (p.32). She has little love for life. (See the bottom of page 26.) Her dream (p.34) – which extends the dream she has after Tia takes her dress (p.11) – suggests how little strength she has to protect herself against the marriage that her stepfather can arrange now that the convent has made her docile.

Do you see how the convent episode has not merely filled in the surface of the story, but revealed how the forces of religion and the patriarchal family combine to determine the future course of a young woman who has already been made vulnerable by the operation of historical, economic and political circumstances beyond her control? I deliberately made that last sentence as dry as possible to remind you that the novelist (unlike the critic) does not work in abstractions, but represents ideas and values in the imaginary forms of people, places and things – as you will find if you reread the novel from the beginning. Try to find half an hour to do this before going on.

There is not sufficient space to continue with the very detailed guidance on reading the novel that I have provided up to this point. In any case I hope by now you feel ready for a more independent reading. In the next section of the unit I've set out some deliberately searching (and leading) questions, which are designed to help you build on the work you have done so far when you move on to study Parts Two and Three of the novel. The questions highlight some of the novel's major themes and thinking about them should equip you to evaluate the more discursive arguments about the novel and its significance in Sections 4 and 5 of this unit.

# 3  PARTS TWO AND THREE

## Part Two

It could be said that the historical forces that combine to bring about the burning of Coulibri are enough to drive anyone mad, and that is what happens to Annette. In writing the novel as she did, Rhys was repudiating on behalf of her ancestry the slander that all Creoles are degenerate, and that their madness is inherited as a consequence of 'bad' breeding. Even Frances Wyndham, in the first introduction to this novel (reproduced as an Appendix to the Penguin edition, pp.125–30), felt able to write of 'mad Creole heiresses ... products of an inbred, decadent society' (p.129). Both Wyndham and the fictional characters who represent this slanderous viewpoint assume that madness is in the Creole blood like a latent virus. Antoinette's husband, in the second and longest part of the novel, is more suspicious of 'out breeding' (with black people). However, I want you to look for the ways in which this novel shows that it is external rather than inherent forces that drive people mad.

Part Two contains twenty short sections of text and for convenience in the discussion below I have numbered these i–xx. As you read Part Two, I suggest that at the end of each section you pause and make the very briefest of notes about who encounters whom, what happens and any themes that strike you. You can use this to provide key words that will help you find your way around the novel, for example when writing an assignment. For about three-quarters of this part of the novel I have provided key words that seem appropriate – although you can add to them or disagree – but thereafter I have left you to do this for yourself.

Within each section, the areas of the novel to which the questions refer are identified by page numbers. Of course, you shouldn't read solely to find answers to the questions. There will be points of your own you want to record and passages to mark because they impress you in some way. Nor should you feel you have to *respond* to all the questions. These are the kinds of question that your tutor might ask to get a discussion going, even though they may not have clear-cut answers.

You should use the notes at the end of the Penguin edition of the novel for clarification as you read. You'll notice that I do not refer to Antoinette's husband by name because Rhys does not name him, even though this is sometimes awkward. I do this to remind you that he is not Brontë's Mr Rochester, but an independent creation. However, other critics often call him Mr Rochester for convenience, as they do in TV23.

Before you start, I want to return to a simple but crucial point I made towards the end of Section 2: 'the novelist ... represents ideas and values in the imaginary forms of people, places and things'. In that section we concentrated on developing the skills involved in reading a novel closely. Although in this section you should continue to read with due care and attention, I would like you now to learn how to stand back and take in more of the novel's overall structure and patterns.

To see how structure and pattern are constructed, we can start by developing the statement above: 'the novelist suggests significance by deploying these imaginary forms in ways that invite comparison or contrast'. This needs some consideration. Tia and Antoinette are 'imaginary forms'. The story deploys them in such a way that we can see the contrasts and comparisons between them. An arrangement in pairs of contrasting opposites is one of the simplest of patterns, and this novel is packed with such pairs. Black and white, ex-slaves and slave-owners, old planters and newcomers are just three we have already encountered. Each side of these pairs throws the other into relief and deepens our understanding by contrast. Look out for more examples of this as you read on because we shall be returning to it later.

## EXERCISE

Now read Part Two (pp.39–112), and then go back and work through it section by section in conjunction with the text below.  ∎

### i     Arrival – Antoinette, husband, servants – strangers

Page

39     Whose is this new point of view?

       Notice especially in the first few pages the new narrator's attitude to the place, people and their language.

What words and phrases suggest an unpropitious start to a honeymoon?

40   Compare the new narrator's description of Antoinette's racial descent with Antoinette's thoughts about her mother's background on page 18. What does this new narrator feel about his wife?

## ii   Journey – arrival – more servants – Christophine – letter to his father

42   What is the basis of this marriage and in what ways does it resemble slavery?

43   Look at the references to England and Englishness here: in connection with Antoinette's appearance, the soil and the 'imitation ... summer house'. Do you see how, despite her husband's wish to find likenesses of home, what is implied is that all these things, like Antoinette's descent (p.40), are 'not English'.

44–5   What does Antoinette's husband's reaction to his frangipani wreath suggest about him? Is his reaction to the tropical landscape the same?

45   How does he think of his dressing-room? Does the feeling last? Compare Antoinette's feelings about Coulibri (p.12) and the convent (pp.31–2). What are the menaces that make both of them need a place of safety?

## iii   Flashback – courtship and wedding – Antoinette's fears

46–8   Why do you think the only thing Antoinette's husband remembers about his wedding is the 'memorial tablets' to the slave-owners?

What have you learned so far in Part Two about her husband's reasons for marrying Antoinette?

## iv   First night at Granbois – England – reality and dreams – Antoinette's memory of rats

48–9   At the beginning of the brief period of the couple's greatest harmony, which exchange of impressions best defines the extent of their difference?

50–1   What do you make of Antoinette's strange waking-dream about the rats? Compare her dreams on pages 11 and 34. Do her dreams suggest that she is irrational or that she has an intuitive perception of the dangers around her?

### v    Breakfast – husband's attitude to Christophine – dirty – lazy – sexy

52–3    Compare Antoinette's husband's attitude to Christophine with Mason's to black people on pages 27–8 and 30. Like her mother, Antoinette claims a better understanding of black people, but in the light of Antoinette's failed friendship with Tia, how complete do you think that understanding is?

### vi    The bathing-pool – 'alien … loveliness' – snakes – crabs

54    Sandi has made just one brief appearance on page 28, so don't think you've missed something. The text does not include any passage where this 'coloured relative' taught Antoinette to throw. Notice, however, that this short episode is packed with secrets, and things hidden or uncertain.

Now that you have read quite a lot of Antoinette's husband's point of view, let's pause and take stock of him. First, did you notice that his narrative is half of one of the contrasting pairs I referred to earlier? His point of view throws hers into relief. You might well have added 'husband and wife' and/or 'male and female' to the list.

What do you make of this man? A cold man, I'd say, who has married a stranger for her money and can hardly find an ungrudging word to say about her, her beautiful island or her household. Every positive impulse is followed by a negative reaction.

Do you recall the comparison I suggested between 'elusive' and 'solid' characterization (p.180 above)? Antoinette's husband is a complex character but he is more predictable than Antoinette. It may help you to think of him as Rhys's critical version of a familiar stereotype: the strong, silent hero of all kinds of romantic fiction, from Mills & Boon to westerns. Antoinette's husband isn't exactly silent, but he is very 'buttoned-up', with a stiff upper lip. If you see him in relation to a stereotype, it will help you to remember that he, like everything else in a novel, is a *construction*: something that the author has made up.

### vii    Loneliness – distrust of servants – night – death – sex – England

54–9    'A short youth mine was' says Antoinette's husband on page 51, and the beginnings of its end are discernible in this section. Notice how notes of difference and threat mark the acceleration of the couple's sexual passion until it becomes almost indistinguishable from the death Antoinette has craved before, and eventually violent. At least, that seems to me what is hinted. Do you agree? And if there is madness here, who is mad? At the beginning of Section 3 above, I suggested that Rhys may see what is thought of as madness as an understandable response to intolerable circumstances. Would that be the case here?

viii    Cosway's letter – slavery – interbreeding – madness

59–62   Is there any reason to think Daniel Cosway's account of Antoinette's family history is more reliable than what we have previously been told?

ix    Amélie turns on Antoinette – who strikes her – Christophine leaving – threatens Amélie – black/white – 'Where do I belong'

63–4   Do you think Amélie has had her eye on Antoinette's husband from the beginning? (See page 39.) Why might she be attracted to him – sex, money, power or all three?

Is Antoinette helpless without her black nurse? (See pages 9, 11, 14–15.)

x    Hides his feelings – rum and sleep

64   What is proverbially British about the husband here?

xi    Gets lost – obeah – zombis

67   Notice how the rational husband looks up an authoritative explanation for what has just happened, including Baptiste's obstinacy.

xii    Change of narrator – Antoinette visits Christophine – C's advice – England – love-potion – Aunt Cora – money

68   What advice does Christophine give?

69   Why does Antoinette reject it?

Which woman lives outside the law and which is the victim of law?

xiii    Cosway's second letter – Amélie's account of him – Sandi

76   What is Amélie's opinion of Daniel Cosway? Do you think her version of events is reliable? (There are similarities here with the question in section viii above.)

xiv    Visit to Cosway – epitaphs – accuses Christophine of obeah – Sandi – interbreeding

77–8   Although there are ostensibly only two narrators (Antoinette and her husband) the novel includes several more 'points of view' which have their own distinctive voices. Can you list them?

79–80    Is her husband more worried about the possibility that Antoinette has inherited insanity – or that she has inherited black genes?

### xv    Now list the remaining key words yourself

82    Her husband makes Antoinette promise to be 'reasonable'. Is that what her story is?

86–7    The name 'Bertha' is another detail from *Jane Eyre*, where the mad wife is called Bertha Antoinetta Mason.

87    Would it be fair to say that the tragedy becomes more painful because at this moment it seems as though it might have been averted?

### xvi    List your key words here

89–90    What do you think of Antoinette's husband's morning-after reaction to Amélie?

91–2    Whom has he identified as his real enemy and how does he try to deal with her?

### xvii    List your key words here

94    Antoinette calls justice 'a cold word'. Make a note of earlier references to the law (for example, pages 11 and 69) and look out for further instances.

95    Antoinette is crazy with drink but is she insane?

97–8    How does Christophine react to violence? How do the new doctors react?

98–9    What Antoinette's husband calls Christophine's 'judge's voice' is echoed by his own reflections. Do you see how his voice when he speaks directly has a harsh, cold quality not shared by the voice that echoes in his head, so that at this point he becomes divided, and his sureness of identity collapses?

102    The italics in parentheses refer back to Daniel Cosway's parting speech when Antoinette's husband visited his house (p.80). What insinuations have fatally turned Antoinette's husband against her?

103–4    Is insanity the real issue, or property and power?

### xviii    List your key words here

104–5    Who's Antoinette's husband blaming now?

### xix    List your key words here

106–7    And who's mad now? Why do you think this section is marked off by asterisks?

## xx    List your key words here

108    In a moment of belated regret, Antoinette's husband still blames the 'black snake-like forest'. What are the real causes of his wretchedness?

108–12  Do you recall the term 'stream of consciousness'? Here the stream passes through a variety of moods and tones. What do you think Antoinette's husband has learned by the end of it?

FIGURE 23.3  *Dominica: the other side of the world from the English setting for* Jane Eyre. *(Photograph: Cicely Palser Havely)*

# Part Three

As this short final part of the novel purports to be the vision of a madwoman, you should not expect it to make perfect sense. The 'Notes to the Text' reveal that it ties in more closely with *Jane Eyre*. Although the details are unimportant, you may find it reassuring to be told a little more of the plot of the earlier novel. Bertha Antoinetta Mason, Mr Rochester's mad wife, is guarded by a servant, Grace Poole. When Bertha's stepbrother Richard Mason comes from the West Indies to visit her, she attacks him and it is then that Jane Eyre learns of her presence in the attic. Jane only finds out that Bertha is Rochester's wife when she is about to marry him herself. Eventually Bertha sets fire to the house (something she has attempted before). Rochester is blinded trying to rescue her from the flames but she dies jumping from the battlements. Her death frees Rochester for marriage to Jane.

Bertha never speaks in Brontë's novel (and Jane never appears in Rhys's). Bertha's predicament provided the title for a highly regarded work of feminist literary criticism: *The Mad Woman in the Attic: the woman writer and the nineteenth-century literary imagination* (1979) by Sandra Gilbert and Susan Gubar. There it is suggested that Bertha represents suppressed female rage and power, and that she is in a sense the silenced part of Jane (and of 'Everywoman').

### EXERCISE

Now read Part Three (pp.115–24). Then work through it section by section, making notes to provide key words and using the questions as guidance as you did for Part Two. ■

### i        List your key words here

Page

115      Here's another point of view. Is the house a prison to all the women it contains?

### ii, iii    List your key words here

117      Do you recall Antoinette looking at another child as if she were her own reflection in a mirror?

### iv       List your key words here

117, 118 What makes Antoinette doubt that she is in England?

### v, vi     List your key words here

120–1    Sandi is mentioned again, although we still aren't allowed to piece together a reliable version of the story. Do you think there can ever be a totally reliable story told by a person recounting his or her own experience?

vii    List your key words here

122    This dream concludes the sequence begun on pages 11 and 34 as it merges into Antoinette's present 'reality' and future ending. As you read the last couple of pages notice how 'the flight of steps leads to this room' (p.122) – that is, how the 'steps' of her life, which are recalled by phrase after phrase echoing the earlier stages of the novel, have brought her to this plight.

Of course, none of us reads this carefully all the time, but as *The Arts Good Study Guide* shows you, it is possible to become a better reader most of the time and a very good reader when you need to be. You most need to be a good reader when you are going to say something about what you have read or compare your own opinions with someone else's. If you're not too pressed for time, you could read carefully through the Introduction to the Penguin edition of the novel (pp.vii–xxiii), because you are now in a better position to decide whether you agree with its opinions.

In the two final sections of this unit, we are going to return to some of the recurrent themes of this block. The aim is first to re-emphasize that works of art are produced in a cultural and historical *context*, and that each relates to the *traditions* and practices of its genre. The exploration and re-working of familiar *myths* will also be noted. In the concluding section we will look at the treatment of *race* and *gender* in *Wide Sargasso Sea* from a perspective that you will be able to apply, not just to other texts in this block and this course, but in a wide range of situations where these important issues are encountered.

# 4  CONTEXT, TRADITION AND MYTHS

One of the reasons for choosing this novel was that it reminds its readers, in a particularly striking way, that no work of art stands alone. It proceeds from a cultural tradition and will go on to contribute to the development of that tradition. The parts of *Jane Eyre* that have most bearing on Rhys's novel are parts that many readers skip, because Rochester's account of his first marriage is overblown and unconvincing, and because they're impatient to know whether Jane will stay with her beloved master now that their wedding has been dramatically prevented by the disclosure of a mad wife in the attic.

However, when Rhys read *Jane Eyre* she didn't skip Rochester's account, because she had been born to white planters in Dominica. This Caribbean island's history, culture and landscape are discussed in TV23. Rhys knew that Brontë 'was wrong ... her Bertha is impossible' (undated letter to Francis Wyndham, 1964, *Jean Rhys: Letters 1931–1966*, 1985, p.271). Indeed, Brontë, the spinster daughter of a Yorkshire vicar, whose knowledge of foreign parts was limited to a period of living in Brussels, might well write unconvincingly about lust and madness in the tropics. Rhys, with her vivid childhood memories of Dominica, was troubled not only by the unlikely descriptions in *Jane Eyre* but also by the unfairness and one-sided perspective of a classic Victorian novel, which just about every English-language-educated novel-reader of her generation would have read, not just in Britain but throughout its world-wide empire.

You may not think of the English language and its literature as one of Britain's most politically significant exports, but from the beginning of the nineteenth century British governments systematically educated an élite in every major colony to think like their rulers. This was part of what came to be known as Britain's 'civilizing mission', but in effect it was part of a more cynical process of rendering the indigenous population more governable. School textbooks, journals and periodicals of all kinds, histories, poetry and novels all contributed to this massive cultural indoctrination, which can be compared with the spread of American culture since World War II. In TV23, the historian Lennox Honychurch remembers how thoroughly British and incongruous was the education he received in Dominica during the 1950s and 1960s.

## EXERCISE

Where in *Wide Sargasso Sea* do you recall incongruous traces of Englishness, or unreliable ideas about England? Here, the keyword index to Parts Two and Three you have prepared should help you in what is not a very easy novel to find your way around.

## DISCUSSION

Any miller's daughter in the Caribbean would surely be black-eyed, not blue-eyed. Antoinette's 'favourite picture' (p.18) is a work of 'chocolate-box' art, and, like the rest of Coulibri, it is destroyed by the recently freed slaves. Just as Mason's English ideas about the Caribbean are all wrong (pp.17–18), so are Antoinette's about England, a mythical place where she hopes her helpless brother will be cured (p.18).

This mutual misunderstanding continues in Antoinette's marriage. Both she and her husband think the other's country is a dream (p.49), although again it is the Englishman who insists that his own view is right: 'About England ... her fixed ideas would never change' (p.58). Her England is a never-never myth, created out of a mishmash of rote-learning and romantic fiction (p.70). Christophine's picture of England is just as imaginary, although she is more sceptical (p.70).

Antoinette is torn between fantasies of England and the pull of her birthplace, just as her husband is both lured and menaced by what he sees as the alien beauty of the Caribbean. But his Englishness is also constructed, not inborn. He learned to hide his feelings at a tender age (p.64) and Englishness is always his point of reference (p.43). Both have been made what they are by the culture, the education, the historical circumstances and even the climate in which they were raised.

Don't worry if you didn't recall all of these examples. One or two would be enough to make the point.

---

There is a symmetry in *Wide Sargasso Sea* which corrects the one-sided account in *Jane Eyre*. Brontë saw the wealth and sensuality of the tropical colonies as a place of moral danger to the Englishman, but Rhys reveals not just the other side of the coin, but both sides simultaneously. Her novel has two main points of view – and, indeed, others beside, for we are made aware that the black and mixed-blood West Indians could tell their stories too.

Although it is Block 6 that addresses the 1960s, the material in this unit is also relevant to a study of that period. Rhys's novel was set in the 1830s but it was largely written during the 1960s, and was shaped by, and itself helped to shape, the culture of that time. Literature in the post-war period in Britain was preoccupied with the state of a recovering nation: if you haven't read them, you may have seen the films made of John Braine's novel *Room at the Top* (1957) or John Osborne's play *Look Back in Anger* (1956). On this rather drab scene, a work like *Wide Sargasso Sea* seemed to open a window onto the possibilities of worlds elsewhere. Not only was the setting of the novel so gorgeously exotic, its form opened up all kinds of possibility about what the novel could do. It wasn't alone, of course, and some of you who are already literature fans might remember the extraordinary impact of the Brazilian Gabriel Garcia Marquez's novel *One Hundred Years of Solitude,* which was originally published in 1967, although it wasn't translated into English until 1970.

You'll already be aware from Block 1, from your work on art history in Block 3 and from this block that, whilst the creative arts have their own traditions, they are also shaped by historical forces, even when the precise relationship is hard to define. *Wide Sargasso Sea* has an acknowledged literary ancestor, but its other imaginative source was thousands of miles away, in a region from which the West and North America expected nothing to come but trouble. The 1950s and 1960s were the era of substantial immigration to Britain from its (former) West Indies colonies and 1967 was the year in which the conservative MP Enoch Powell made a notoriously xenophobic speech predicting riot and rivers of blood. Racism, you might reflect, depends on stereotypical 'myths' about different cultures. As Rhys shows, we all create myths about other people, and as Arthur Marwick pointed out in Unit 8, myths are powerful enough to create wars.

During the second half of the eighteenth century and throughout the nineteenth and early twentieth centuries, European colonialism had obliterated, ignored or at best devalued local cultures, in Britain's case systematically effacing them with its own 'civilizing mission'. Most Victorian literature had reflected a world-view in which Britain was at the centre and all other points of view were marginalized. But as the old imperial powers retreated after World War II (or 'granted independence'), long-suppressed voices began to emerge, in art, music and literature as well as more obvious political action. A landmark example is the Nigerian novelist's Chinua Achebe's *Things Fall Apart* (1958), which tells the story of an African culture's crucial first encounter with white missionaries. By the second half of the 1990s, when I write this, the literary map has changed, and continues to change, just as the political map has changed. 'English' (in the sense of 'made in England') literature now looks like a rather small and possibly unimportant part of global literary output. Salman Rushdie described the international literary surge in which he is himself such a notable figure as 'the Empire writes back to the Centre' – a punning reference to the second of the 1970s *Star Wars* movies, *The Empire Strikes Back.* By 'the Centre' Rushdie meant not so much the British, or the colonizer, or even the English-speaking world, as that vague, vast, self-important constituency which assumes itself, in a 1960s phrase, 'to be where it's at'. Anyone who has inherited an assumption (no matter how unconscious) that he or she is at 'the Centre' is bound to see everyone else as more or less peripheral or marginal.

Throughout this block, we've considered some of the ways in which works of art can grow out of an artistic tradition and feed into subsequent works. They are also, we keep repeating, a product of their historical as well as their artistic circumstances. Although it is not always clear that any work of art can 'make a difference', here I want to suggest that *Wide Sargasso Sea* has contributed to a shift in political thinking. The novel has sometimes been described as the 'first of the prequels', and it is certainly prominent amongst recent re-workings and alternative versions of taken-for-granted classics. 'Red Riding Hood' has been re-told from the wolf's point of view, *Hamlet* from the courtiers', and *Robinson Crusoe* from Man Friday's, among others (Angela Carter, *The Company of Wolves*, 1984; Tom Stoppard, *Rosencrantz and Guildenstern are Dead*, 1966; J.M. Coetze, *Foe*, 1986). The collective importance of such alternatives and of all artistic production from a previously suppressed perspective is that they challenge conventional, blinkered perspectives (such as ideas about race and gender), which often become so ingrained that we think they are natural and inevitable.

At the beginning of this block (Unit 19, p.29), I pointed out that the word 'myth' may be used to mean a story widely held to be true which turns out not to be true. Ideas that are repeated so often that they pass unchallenged will often coalesce into a kind of myth. We noticed, for example, how the seeming laziness of freed slaves became solidified into a stereotype. *Wide Sargasso Sea* debunks a whole cluster of British myths about the Caribbean colonies, including, it has to be said, the treasured myth that emancipation was an unalloyed triumph of enlightened benevolence. It is a myth that women are 'naturally' liable to madness, rather than driven to it by circumstances, or that Creole colonies are 'degenerate'. It's a myth that jungles are evil. The structure of Rhys's novel allows us to break free from a one-sided perspective and see that those who judge others according to myths and stereotypes are themselves liable to the same reductive treatment.

# 5  RACE, GENDER AND 'DIFFERENCE'

In another sense, myths are traditional stories that writers, artists and musicians re-work for their own ends, but, as in the case of all the works considered in this block, such re-workings often entail a critical analysis of the myth and its significance. At about the same time that *Wide Sargasso Sea* was being written, the black Civil Rights Movement in the United States was helping to fuel a new wave of feminist activity, which had been relatively dormant since the suffrage movements early in the century. The oppression of women by men can be seen as analogous with the oppression of black people by white, and 'Women's Lib' became a political slogan almost contemporaneous with black freedom. I'm jumping the gun again, but another reason to look back at *Wide Sargasso Sea* from the 1960s perspective of the next block will be because its insistence on expressing a previously silenced voice makes it in its way a 'liberationist' text and even a product of the counter-culture.

If you look back to page 173 in Section 2 of this unit you'll find the statement that the 'adult speech registers *difference*'. On page 174 I spoke of the '*white characters' difference*' and on page 175 of Christophine as being 'different'. On page 179 Tia is called '*different*'. Why did I keep hammering home this perfectly ordinary word? Because 'difference' is a key word in the analysis of both race and gender, and because, as we have seen, *Wide Sargasso Sea* is organized into a series of opposites, which may be as alike as reflections in a mirror and yet intractably different. Look at the moment when Tia throws the stone:

> I did not feel it ... only something wet, running down my face. I looked at her and I saw her face crumple up as she began to cry. We stared at each other, blood on my face, tears on hers. It was as if I saw myself. Like in a looking glass.

> *(p.24)*

'Difference' is what divides us, but the related concept of 'otherness', which has its roots in Freudian psychology, claims that the sense of self we need to survive in a modern society is partly created by emphasizing what is not-self, or other. Since World War II, this has been refined to analyse various complex social phenomena. The pioneering French feminist Simone de Beauvoir revealed in *The Second Sex* (1953) how women are habitually represented as not-men, or other-than-men. Since then, all kinds of liberationists have identified their oppressors as having a perspective that sees them as different or *other than* the supposed norm. But the oppressor may also view what is conceived of as 'the other' with fear generated by the perceived difference between them. Thus Europe, politically dominant since the seventeenth century, saw the 'other' worlds where it raided and traded as mysterious and frightening and, by extension, as feminine, that is, luxurious, indulgent and debilitating: all the things that the virile invader was *not*.

This, roughly speaking, was the conclusion of *Orientalism* (1978), a seminal work of cultural and historical synthesis by the Palestinian scholar Edward Said (pronounced Sy-eed). The Orient, he suggests, is not so much a geographical region as an imaginary realm constructed by the dominant powers out of self-justification. Although it is vast in its scope, *Orientalism* is nevertheless mostly limited to European scholarly, descriptive and fictional writings about Asia. But Said's thesis can be applied to many other imaginary constructions, such as 'darkest Africa', 'the evil Empire' or 'tropical paradise', which compress what is alien into simplistic generalizations.

## EXERCISE

Check these ideas against the picture you have of Antoinette's husband. Is his Caribbean 'an imaginary realm'? Is he a representative of 'the dominant powers'? Is his attitude one of 'self-justification'? Does he see the island as 'feminine ... luxurious, indulgent and debilitating'?

## DISCUSSION

I would hardly expect you to answer 'No'. My thumb was in the scale. Although Antoinette's husband experiences the island as a dream (p.49), the menace he feels in the landscape is almost entirely imaginary. The local black people disconcert him, but he always expects to dominate, because he has money, the law and assumed racial superiority on his side. He blames his wife, the servants, his father, Richard Mason – anyone but himself. And whilst he hates the place, he is also seduced by it.

In all kinds of ways, *Wide Sargasso Sea* is written 'from the other side' – the other side of Jane Eyre's story, the other side of the world, the other side of sanity. Do you see how the main contrasts in the structural patterns of the novel combine to convey a sense of multiple opposites, always illuminating each other and always in tension? In an article that reintroduced Rhys to the literary world in 1964, Wyndham wrote of her 'passion for stating the case of the underdog' (Wyndham, 1964). This was to be just as evident in *Wide Sargasso Sea*, still incomplete at the time, where former slaves and their descendants and women both black and white are oppressed by the white male ruling class. Although the black characters defy their oppressors and begin to lay claim to their freedom, the two main white women in the novel, Antoinette and her mother, both succumb to incarceration, humiliation and madness.

As Creole women in the historical circumstances of this novel, there is really nowhere they are at home. Poverty, her French Martinique origins and her first husband's scandalous reputation (p.13) alienate Annette and her daughter from the respectable, gossiping English ladies of Jamaica, who equally despise the new English entrepreneur whom she marries. The freed black people hate the newcomers who take advantage of the economic collapse that followed emancipation, because as Christophine says: 'Same thing ... New ones worse than old ones – more cunning that's all' (p.11). So great is the difference between both women and their English husbands that they seem in some ways closer to the black people with whom socially and culturally they have so little in common. Annette (like Aunt Cora) claims a relatively greater understanding of her black servants and their community than her husband, even though she fears and despises them (pp.15–16, 17–18).

Unlike her mother, Antoinette wants – even yearns – to cross the racial and cultural divide, and at one level the beginning of her childhood friendship with Tia might be thought potentially capable of transcending the differences of the adult world. But on another level it raises the difficult question of whether racial and gender 'differences' can ever be obliterated. Certainly, the friendship ends. Tia is in tears when she throws the stone, but her people have 'closed ranks' (p.5) too, and she has no choice.

*Wide Sargasso Sea* was originally greeted in Britain as if it spoke for the whole Caribbean population – which shows how unconscious white people still were about their supremacist and generalizing tendencies. It was a black West Indian poet, Keanu Braithwaite (1974), who angrily pointed out that 'white creoles in the ... West Indies have separated themselves by too wide a gulf ... to ... identify or be identified with' the authentic Caribbean experience. By this time, American Black Power politics were rousing the Caribbean, and Braithwaite was angered by the assumption that the daughter of privileged white planters, no matter how impoverished, could understand the point of view of a black person.

In fact, I don't think Rhys does pretend to speak on behalf of her black characters. If you look carefully, she never attempts to get 'inside' their experience, in the way she speaks through Antoinette and her husband. (Some people would argue that it is as inappropriate for a woman to write from a man's point of view as for a white person to impersonate someone black. In my opinion that way lies imaginative sterility, although there's no space to pursue the argument here.) Nowadays the majority of critics argue that Rhys's work reflects not the whole history of the Caribbean (how could it?) but her circumscribed experience as a woman, a Creole and an expatriate.

In Section 2 I asked you to consider both the explicit and implicit racism in this text. Neither of the fictional children nor their creator can escape from the ideology that their cultures and histories have imprinted upon them. But if we do not know, and do not pretend to know, what another person is thinking, that 'other' tends to be defined as 'unknowable' (or 'enigmatic' or 'inscrutable'), which in itself tends towards a racist position. It's a 'no-win situation'. Antoinette's husband feels threatened because he cannot understand the black servants. Even after he has sexually penetrated Amélie, he does not know her any better. *It is not only black and white who are separated by this gulf of unknowability. In Rhys's view, men and women are seen as equally alien to each other. It is not madness that divides them but existential loneliness.*

It is good practice, when you find yourself making a broad statement like this, to go back to the text and see if detailed consideration will bear it out or modify it. So I want now to look at *why* Antoinette and her husband are so 'alien'. When we are reintroduced to Antoinette in her husband's narration in Part Two, one of the first things we notice is how socialized she is – perhaps as a result of her schooling. She greets the inhabitants of Massacre and the servants at Granbois like friends; she's affectionate and exuberant with her new husband: 'This is my place and everything is on our side', she says (p.45). The way her husband tells it, she seems to have crossed the racial divide that separated her from Tia, and made friends. He, on the other hand, is cautious and inhibited. There's a consistent rhythm to his responses and reactions to both people and place. He is first attracted then corrects himself. Amélie is first a 'lovely little creature' then 'spiteful, malignant perhaps, like much else in this place' (p.39). He is laughed at, cried at, lied to, seen through – and won't enter Caro's house, even to get out of the rain (pp.40–1). He cannot admit that his wife's hat is becoming without subsequently adding that her eyes are 'too large ... disconcerting ... alien' (p.40). One of the porters has 'A magnificent body' but 'a foolish conceited face' (p.41). The negative rationalization of an instinctive response is ingrained. At Granbois he first surrenders to the 'intoxicating freshness' (p.44) of its exotic fragrance, then steps on the wreath and fills the room with 'the scent of crushed flowers' (p.45). The letter he drafts to his father is a message back to the orderly, dull, regulated world he has left behind. It's second nature to him to put what is new and different at a distance, not a defect of character for which he can be blamed or from which he might easily escape. He has been programmed to maintain his male, English predominance by resisting even the challenge of his own senses.

It may well be that Antoinette's much friendlier although ambivalent attitudes to Afro-Caribbeans are a kind of fellow-feeling in a woman who has quite blatantly been sold in marriage. But although she is well disposed to them, she is not immune to the inherently racist habit of labelling people she professes to understand, and the more she insists on her familiarity, the more aloof her husband's reaction:

> 'They don't care about getting a dress dirty because it shows it isn't the only dress they have. Don't you like Christophine?'
>
> 'She is a very worthy person no doubt. I can't say I like her language.'
>
> *(pp.52–3)*

Her labels ('The girls here are very shy', p.56) may be kinder than her mother's accusations of inertia and self-interest (p.8), but they generalize and diminish none the less. What's more, she fiercely resists the corresponding labels for her own family: 'so without a doubt not English, but no white nigger either. Not my mother. Never had been. Never could be' (p.18). Later, insulted by Amélie and thinking herself deserted by Christophine, her own momentary acknowledgement of such humiliating labels is confused with a snobbish claim to right of settlement and a racist slur:

> 'a white cockroach. That's me. That's what they call all of us who were here before their own people in Africa sold them to the slave traders. And I've heard English women call us white niggers. So between you I often wonder who I am and where is my country and where do I belong and why was I ever born at all.'
>
> *(p.64)*

Alienation (and the rum) makes her defensively aloof, unjust and bitter. So they are *both* alienated; you could even say that they are alike in their isolation.

## EXERCISE

Where in this block have you previously considered the alienation of a character? Was it anything to do with race and/or gender?

## DISCUSSION

It's hard to say whether, in the past, works of art have merely recorded gendered differences or actually helped to create them. Something of both, no doubt. *Pygmalion* jokes about the incomprehensible unreasonableness of women and the obtuseness of men; *Don Juan* allocates different musical languages to men and women. But it is in

*Medea*, of course, that gender combines with race as mutually alienating factors to make Medea doubly outcast.

---

*Wide Sargasso Sea* is so much more than an explanation of how the mad wife in *Jane Eyre* reached the attic. It is a critique of what is inherently contradictory in the imperial enterprise. Commercial opportunism throughout the history of the Empire was always laced with the inadmissible lure of the exotic and the erotic, but Victorian respectability and the Protestant work ethic managed to smother the glamour and romance in denying the exploitation, and re-packaged the endeavour as the 'white man's burden' and Britain's 'civilizing mission' to the less fortunate parts of the globe. To succumb to the sensual charms of the Caribbean (or India, or Africa) or to blend in with its culture was to attract the accusation of 'going native'. What is enjoyed must be despised: 'In the morning, of course, I felt differently' about Amélie, says Antoinette's husband. 'Another complication. Impossible. And her skin was darker, her lips thicker than I had thought' (p.89). He even resists the landscape, although 'however far I travel I'll never see a lovelier' (p.106). It is not just a 'dream' (p.49) but ultimately a nightmare:

> More than ever before [the shabby white house] strained away from the black snake-like forest. Louder and more desperately it called: Save me from destruction, ruin and desolation. Save me from the long slow death by ants ... Don't you know that this is a dangerous place? And that the dark forest always wins? Always.
>
> *(p.108)*
>
> I hated the mountains and the hills, the rivers and the rain. I hated the sunsets of whatever colour, I hated its beauty and its magic and the secret I would never know. I hated its indifference and the cruelty which was part of its loveliness.
>
> *(p.111)*

The place itself seems to goad Antoinette's husband into overloading it with sinister interpretations. It is dangerous, magic, secret and unknowable. These are the same terms that Joseph Conrad applied to Africa in the most famous of all anti-imperial novels, *Heart of Darkness* (1902). Despite savagely criticizing the squalor and cruelty of colonial exploitation, Conrad's novel identifies metaphysical darkness and horror not with the white man's ravages but with the essential being of Africa: not with his own kind, but with the unknowable 'other'.

This syndrome – the invaders' fears being translated into the unknown territory's hostility – remains familiar in all kinds of popular narratives such as science fiction. What *Wide Sargasso Sea* reveals is that much of that fear emanates from the darkness within the invader, and that its source is not the hostile jungle, but the bitter residues of history. Antoinette's husband suspects that one of those residues is that black and white are all 'probably related' (p.81). So they are, but not necessarily in the blood sense he means.

Daniel Cosway, Antoinette's probable half-brother, who first stirs her husband's guilt into suspicious hatred, is in a sense *his* brother too. Both are betrayed by their fathers, both resort to dishonourable ways of making money. Like Tia and Antoinette, they are mirror opposites, both identical and opposed. The novel is full of such reflections: Annette and Antoinette, Mason and Antoinette's husband, perhaps Aunt Cora and Christophine. Antoinette and her husband are opposite sides of the same coin – both perhaps minted by slavery. Perhaps Coulibri had to be destroyed as Antoinette's husband's English house must be burned because both, although beautiful in their opposite ways, were built on the same foundation of slavery. This is a tragic story in which – as in *Medea* – social, cultural and historical forces destroy the lives of those who struggle with them.

But I wonder if a more hopeful reading is possible. We have looked at the pervasive presence of 'difference' and alienation in the novel, but might it not also be possible to see the equally pervasive echoes and reflections as suggesting the reconciliation of difference? After all, although the child reflected in the mirror cannot be kissed (p.117) she can be approached. There can be hope in a mirror (p.5) as well as despair. Reflections suggest likenesses across the divide, and the perception of likeness between oneself and others leads to self-knowledge. So the friendship with Tia breaks down, and Tia must throw the stone, but it is Tia who weeps and Antoinette, the slave-owner's daughter, who sees her own reflection in the child of slaves. At the end of the novel, it is Tia who challenges her in her dream to leap into the pool at Coulibri once more (p.123): 'I called "Tia!" and jumped and woke.' In *Jane Eyre* that leap ends in death, but in *Wide Sargasso Sea* it doesn't end at all.

The imitation of madness allows Rhys to escape from rational explanations and consequences. Antoinette wakes from a dream to enact it, but she doesn't die: at least, not within the narrative – for how can 'I' write the story of 'my' own death? There's a film, famous in the early 1990s, which you may have seen: *Thelma and Louise*. At the end, the two heroines, whom we do not want to die, have no choice but to drive their car over the edge of the Grand Canyon. The film ends with them suspended in mid air. Reason tells us that they're going to hit the bottom, but the credits roll before it happens. Antoinette's narrative ends in a comparable suspense, and in the very last words of the novel the opposites of light and darkness are reconciled in an escape to – what? Death? Coulibri? Tia? 'the flame flickered and I thought it was out. But I shielded it with my hand and it burned up again to light me along the dark passage' (p.124).

What's more, although the novel is a tragedy for its main protagonists, what must not be overlooked is how ineffective is Antoinette's husband's contempt against all others apart from his wife. What he has the power to destroy is not what is 'out there' but only his own intimate happiness. On parting, Baptiste retains 'Not a trace of the polite domestic' (p.108). He has long ago stopped saying 'sir' or 'master' (p.91). Amélie's departure is confident and dignified (p.90). The only black person to be distressed by the couple's departure is the previously unnoticed child who cries 'For nothing' (p.112). Christophine, Antoinette's 'other' mother, is feared, reviled and imprisoned by white, rational males because she practises obeah. But she is healer more than a witch (pp.96–104), and a better Christian than the more orthodox characters. It is not she who turns Antoinette into a zombi, and with her 'judge's voice' (p.98) she stands up 'undaunted' (p.104) by threats of police action. She walks away without looking back. Perhaps hers is the real last word.

*

Everyone's reading of this intricate novel will be a little different. This is one of the pleasures of literary study, but it can be unsettling. Whilst the language of analysis – including your essays – must strive for clarity, literary language may revel in its own ambiguity.

You saw in your work on *Medea* that translation must be an art and not a science, because words are too unstable to be exchanged like currency, according to definite rules. You've also encountered the difficulties of rendering one medium in terms of another when it comes to expressing musical or visual effects in paintings. We might think that where the medium of the artefact (in this case a novel) is words in your own language, then describing it in more words should be no problem. But that was one of the reasons for selecting for study a text as challenging as *Wide Sargasso Sea*. When a text gives up its meaning without effort, it can seem as if we must all share the same reading. But even *Winnie the Pooh* can be endlessly re-interpreted. We expect the language of a sonnet to be 'poetic' because it announces itself as something self-consciously fashioned; we've seen that even a naturalistic play is 'wrought' by its playwright and performed by its actors. Novels are just as much artefacts, and this one not only approaches the condition of poetry but even that of drama in its use of voices and contrasts. No one expects to have the last word on a poem, nor can there be any last words about a well-made novel. Despite their differences, historians are ultimately in search of a reading of the past about which they can all agree. Literary readers, on the other hand, are happy to discuss multiple meanings in a text. But they must be *in the text*. There would be no more useful way to round off your introduction to literary study than by reading *Wide Sargasso Sea* from the beginning again to see how my reading has helped you to discover your own.

# GLOSSARY

**ambiguity** language or situation capable of multiple interpretations.

**author** writer or inventor of a text.

**description** verbal or written account of the appearance of landscape or objects, or summary of character.

**idiom** characteristic form of expression specific to a group or individual.

**narrative** process of telling not just what happened (the plot) but the related circumstances (description, comment, dialogue).

**narrator** character invented by the author who purports to be relating the story.

**point of view** restricted imaginary perspective of a character in a novel and his or her partial account of events.

**rhetoric** language designed to impress or persuade.

**stream of consciousness** often ungrammatical or elliptical language which pretends to mimic the flow of unexpressed thought.

# REFERENCES

BRAITHWAITE, K. (1974) *Contradictory Omens: cultural diversity and integration in the Caribbean*, Kingston, University of the West Indies.

GREGG, V.M. (1995) *Jean Rhys's Historical Imagination: reading and writing the Creole*, Chapel Hill, University of North Carolina Press.

*Jean Rhys: Letters 1931–1966* (1985, 2nd edn), ed. F. Wyndham and D. Melly, Harmondsworth, Penguin.

WYNDHAM, F. (1964) 'Introduction', *Art and Literature*, no. 1, March, pp.173–7.

# SUGGESTIONS FOR FURTHER READING

GILBERT, S.M. and GUBAR, S. (1979) *The Madwoman in the Attic: the woman writer and the nineteenth-century literary imagination*, New Haven and London, Yale University Press.

# UNIT 24
# READING WEEK

It is particularly important to complete or consolidate the work of Block 5 during this reading week if you have fallen behind, because the analytic and interpretative skills you have been practising here are an important component of the timed TMA (TMA 08), whilst interdisciplinary perspectives are important to the final TMA (TMA 09) – and both these TMAs are compulsory.

As the course has progressed, we have gradually been elaborating on the relationship between ideas or artefacts and the context in which they are both produced and received. In the case of *Medea*, for example, we have seen that the context in which the play was first produced is vastly different from the context in which we 'receive' it today, and that this complicates the processes of interpretation. Now, in the final block, we move to a period (the 1960s) so recent that it still directly affects some of our institutions and thinking, and indeed may be within the living memory of some of you.

It may help you to prepare if you think of some of the 'sixties' aspects of the text you have just studied. *Wide Sargasso Sea*, you'll remember, was written in the 1960s, even though it is *about* the early nineteenth century. It is a product of the time of writing, and consciously or not reflects many of the concerns of that era – race and gender relations in particular. You may recall that I suggested that 'its insistence on expressing a previously silenced voice' makes it in its way a 'liberationist' text, that is, a call for freedom for an oppressed section of society. Its form too is a kind of protest against the traditional forms of novel-writing. As you study Block 6 you might ask yourself whether this novel is a another product of the 'counter-culture'.

# INDEX TO BLOCK 5

This index includes references to the Colour Plates and Plates in the *Illustration Book*; these are indicated by 'CPl' for Colour Plates, and 'Pl' for Plates.

# AN INTRODUCTION TO THE HUMANITIES

## Block 1   Form and Reading
Study Week 1   Seeing
Study Week 2   Form and Meaning in Poetry: the Sonnet
Study Week 3   Listening to Music
Study Week 4   Reasoning

## Block 2   The Colosseum
Study Week 5   The Colosseum
Study Week 6   The Colosseum Tradition
Study Week 7   Reading Week

## Block 3   History, Classicism and Revolution
Study Weeks 8 and 9   Introduction to History, Part 1: Issues and Methods
Study Weeks 10 and 11   Rousseau and Democracy
Study Week 12   Art, History and Politics: David and Friedrich
Study Week 13   Reading Week

## Block 4   Religion and Science in Context
Study Weeks 14 and 15   Studying Religion
Study Weeks 16 and 17   Here's History of Science
Study Week 18   Reading Week

## Block 5   Myths and Conventions
Study Week 19   Studying *Pygmalion*
Study Weeks 20 and 21   *Medea*
Study Week 22   Expression and Representation in Music: Richard Strauss's *Don Juan*
Study Week 23   Jean Rhys: *Wide Sargasso Sea*
Study Week 24   Reading Week

## Block 6   The Sixties: Mainstream Culture and Counter-culture
Study Weeks 25 and 26   Introduction to History, Part 2: Writing History
Study Week 27   Counter-movements in Science
Study Week 28   Religion and Counter-cultures in the 1960s
Study Week 29   Change and Continuity: Music in the 1960s
Study Week 30   Rothko and Warhol

## Block 7   Looking Back, Looking Forward
Study Weeks 31–2